M000239387

PIGAROO AND THE CODE OF THE WEST

PIGAROO AND THE CODE OF THE WEST

Stories & Essays

DAVE STAMEY

Copyright 2021 by Dave Stamey

HorseCamp Books
PO Box 189
Orange Cove, CA 93646

davestamey.com

Scanning, uploading or distribution of this book without permission is a violation of the author's intellectual property. If you'd like permission to use material from this book (other than for review purposes) please contact the publisher.

First Edition April 2021

Soft Cover ISBN: 978-1-09838-465-4
eBook: ISBN: 978-1-09838-466-1

To the memory of
JOHN HENRY REESE

TABLE OF
CONTENTS

A LESSON IN THE LIVESTOCK BUSINESS

ONE OF MY biggest fears is that my cowboy friends will discover that, when I was a kid, at one point we raised–

Man. It's hard to even write this.

We raised. . . hogs.

Whew. Just looking at that word makes me shudder a little.

It conjures up images of an old barn, and steam rising over farrowing pens bedded with yellow straw, warmed by tin heating lamps in the glittering, razor-edged nights of a Montana winter. Of stumbling in clumsy rubber muck boots through two feet of snow after an escaped barrow pig, trying to chase it back through an open gate, watching it squirt away at the last second, time after time, getting the distinct feeling the little turd was enjoying the game. The squealing and snuffling. The incredibly noxious brown, permeating stench of pig manure.

My father told me it smelled just like money.

Unlike the lowly cow, limited to a single measly calf at a time, a sow could produce two litters in a year—two!—and as many as eleven of the grunting little demons per delivery. A hog was not just a hog, it was a veritable four-legged cash machine.

"Smells just like money, boy."

You're not doing a kid any favors by teaching him to equate money with pig manure. Trust me on this.

The old man saw no point in fiddle-farting around. If you're going to do something, by God, do it. We ended up with two hundred sows, mostly the pink waddling Yorkshire breed, and one enormous Chester White boar named Henry, some 4-H kid's county fair project, who would lean his massive weight against the planks of his pen so we could reach through and scratch his bristled back for him. Henry enjoyed his work, and went after it with enthusiasm. We were going to own the whole state of Montana before we were through.

The old man, need I say, lost his shorts.

It's an old story, of course. Many people trapped in agricultural agonies lost their shorts in those days, due to financial miscalculations, freak weather events, sudden livestock diseases or other acts of God. My father's disaster could not be laid at the feet of any vindictive deity, however. His doom thundered down from a different source, a source that smelled distinctly of brimstone and sulphur.

I believe that the markets were simple, once upon a time. A farmer sold pigs because people enjoy eating them. Everybody likes ham, and everybody loves bacon. Always have, always will, so the market for pigs should remain constant, world without end, hallelujah. Shouldn't it? Maybe I'm naive; maybe things have never been that straightforward. I don't know. What I do know is that something happened up there in Washington, DC, in some dark, mysterious cavern where mysterious people do mysterious things to mess with the world in general and the livestock markets in particular. They conjure and tinker up there, with smoking cauldrons and eyes of newt and bundles of strange herbs thrown into open flames. I suspect there are pointy hats, and a great deal of cackling. What they did remains shrouded in rumor and legend, but it caused the hog market to nose dive, and suddenly the pigs that were going to make our fortune no longer smelled like money. The wind had shifted. They were now not worth the fuel it would take to haul them to the sale—and this was when gasoline was thirty-six cents a gallon, mind you. But haul them we would, because they weren't worth the feed it would take to keep them, either.

Then, out of the smoke and wreckage, the miracle.

Enter the Rich Guy.

He rolled into our driveway one morning, out of nowhere, smiling with large, very white teeth. I don't remember what kind of car he drove, but I'll bet it was a big one. Had he flown through our kitchen window wearing a red cape it would have been no more remarkable, though it would have probably startled our mother. This hero took a look at the ranch, at how close it was to the road into Billings, figured how many little ranchettes he could whittle off to sell to folks who wanted to live in the country and still commute to town, then offered a wad of money that made my father's eyes bug out. My mother, California born and raised, had experienced all she wanted of Montana and its unreasonable weather. She wished to go home. I suspect she told the old man that if he didn't take the offer, she'd beat him to death. With a pig.

He took the offer.

We loaded up the truck, and moved to California. Just like the Clampetts. And promptly hurled ourselves right back into the livestock business.

No hogs, this time. No way. We would play it safe, and stick with what we knew: how to lose money in the cow business.

Real estate in California wasn't the same as real estate in Montana. Just in case you were wondering. In California it was much more expensive, because, apparently, they were not making any more of it. We wound up with only twenty acres on which to operate, most of it on a sand dune. Twenty acres of California sand will grow just enough grass to support half a beef, so your basic cow-calf operation was out of the question.

But, if you build a feedlot, you can run a bunch of 'em.

We hammered together pens and feed bunks using second-hand, splintery lumber, two-by-twelves and two-by-sixes and old railroad ties. We bought a used squeeze-chute, and a scale. We hung medicated back scratchers and dust bags from the oak trees, and stocked up on Terramycin. The old man found a couple of partners, they did some kind of song and dance at the bank, and managed to gather up three hundred head of white-faced, bony-hipped brahmer-cross steers. Three hundred head of cattle in a dry lot on twenty acres can feel a bit cramped. It was very much like having the entire cast of *Riverdance* perform on your kitchen counter. No matter—we were in business.

We went looking for something cheap to feed them.

If cattle could gain 2 ½ pounds a day on sand, things would have been perfect. Alas. Instead, we fed them moldy hay and a molasses supplement called Loomix, which we mixed together using a mechanical chopper contraption rigged to work off the flywheel of an ancient John Deere tractor. You had to open the petcocks to get the tractor engine started, then jump down and close them again before it coughed and stalled. We fed culls from the vegetable packing sheds, broccoli and sugar beets and weird looking carrots that the stores wouldn't buy—cosmetic rejects, carrots that looked as if they were grown next to a nuclear waste dump. We shoveled it all into the feed bunks twice a day. The vegetable culls made those cattle loose and squirty. Believe me—two words you never want to hear together are "projectile," and "manure."

"Smells just like money, boy."

We doctored pink eye, popped warble grubs out of their backs with the mouths of empty soda pop bottles, ran them through the chutes and smeared them with fly dope, shoved boluses down their throats to fight the yellow scours, and did everything else we could to keep them alive and gaining. We went to the sale and bought week-old Holstein drop calves, fed them a powdered milk replacer called Calf Manna out of galvanized buckets with rubber nipples screwed on them, dragged them off and buried them when they died, went back and bought more. Eventually some of them made it, got big enough to be shoved into the pens and fend for themselves with the rest of the herd. We sold a few, bought more, bought more, and bought more. We were going to own the whole state of California before we were through.

Then came 1974.

If you or your family were in the cattle business in 1974, I don't need to tell you what happened. It is a dark moment in the history of the West, ranking up there with the winter of 1886, the invention of the singing cowboy, and the death of John Wayne.

Those pointy-hatted evil wizards in the misty caverns of Washington were at it again. They fired up their cauldrons, threw their herb bundles around and cackled in the smoke, and when the smoke lifted the fed-cattle market had crashed like Evel Knieval at Caesar's Palace. We stood there looking at steers that weren't worth the gas it would take to haul them to the sale. Gas was fifty cents a gallon then.

History repeats itself. Everything moves in circles.

Well... Not everything. Damn it.

We started casting our eyes to the horizon—certain that, any minute now, another big shiny car would pull into the yard, and another caped crusading Rich Guy would leap out, smiling his brilliant smile, and offer to buy the ranch.

Still waiting.

In retrospect, what we should have done was buy more cattle. Because, man, they were really cheap right then.

OVER THE MOUNTAINS

I'D BEEN HIRED for an after-dinner performance at a convention of Australian Shepherd dog enthusiasts in Carson City. Amazing dogs, nice people, long industrial style tables with paper tablecloths and plastic flatware, and your choice of beef or chicken for an entrée, both, as usual in these deals, cooked to the consistency of rawhide. Also on the show with me was a cowboy poet friend of mine named Skeeter, who lived close by and invited me to stay with him afterwards.

Everybody has a friend like Skeeter. Well, all right, maybe you don't, but everybody I know does. He has the disagreeable habit of drinking too much, after which he'll describe for you, in great detail, the darkest moments of his four failed marriages while picking his feet over the coffee table. I didn't want to stay with Skeeter. I made the Australian Shepherd folks put me up at a local casino instead.

It turned out they had a budget that was a bit small and cramped, these dog people, and rather than a big, flashy casino—one of those comfortable ones—they put me in a small, cramped place at the edge of town with a small, cramped motel attached. It wasn't the casino with the Beverly Hillbillies theme, but it almost was, and their ventilation system needed work.

Around one o'clock in the morning I woke up, coughing. Something weird had happened with the Casino's fans and airducts, and all the cigarette smoke in the building, which should have been vented to the outside, was now being funneled directly through my room. And that was a bunch of cigarette smoke. It's a Nevada state law that you can't fill out a keno card or pull the lever on a slot machine without smoking a cigarette. Even if you're on oxygen. I've never seen this law written down, but I know it exists, because I've seen the people who obey it, yanking those handles, hacking their lungs out, cigarettes dangling from lower lips, with their oxygen bottles on the floor beside them. This is a tiny and strange facet of Americana that is rarely noted.

I sat up in bed, gasping. I tried opening a window, but you're not allowed to open a motel window in the State of Nevada. There's a law against that, too. Gamblers who lose all their money might try to jump out those windows and commit suicide, even a single-story motel room like the one I was in, where it's only a foot and a half down to the little gravel-and-cactus garden next to the sidewalk. I opened the door to let in some fresh air, and this immediately turned the room into a large, tobacco-smelling ice cube.

And now I was awake. Really awake.

The kind of awake I was is the kind of awake you get when you realize you're not falling back to sleep. Perhaps ever again. You become alert, severely alert, and can suddenly solve complicated math problems, even the one with the guy on the train going thirty miles an hour and walking through the cars at four miles an hour in the opposite direction. You become nervous, and can't sit still. In fact, you feel that if you don't get up and start moving, your brain will short-circuit, and fizzle out.

It was then I arrived at the brilliant idea of getting dressed and driving home. Right now, right this minute.

What a nice surprise it would be for my wife, I thought, when I came rolling through the gate at eight or nine in the morning, instead of my projected late afternoon arrival time. She would be pleased and happy, proud of me for accomplishing such a feat, and I, smart and industrious, would be a hero for finding a way for us to spend more time together.

These are the moments, by the way, that provide me with more material than I can ever possibly use.

I used to know a guy named Roland, who drove a fertilizer truck in Bakersfield. He was an expert on night driving. He never did any night driving himself, but he drove that fertilizer truck every day and, apparently, that will make you tired, in fact wear you plumb out, and he knew what to do about it. His remedy was to drink a cup of coffee, and then, half an hour later, drink a glass of orange juice. This, Roland swore, would get you an hour and a half of being wide awake. An hour and a half exactly. And who am I to argue with an experienced truck driver? Yeah, a fertilizer truck driver, sure—but a truck driver all the same.

I dressed, gathered up my stuff and tossed it into the car. I drove to the nearest AM/PM, where I remembered to buy gas. I always fill my tank before leaving Nevada, because California gas costs more. Much more. I was proud of myself for remembering this—but, you'll recall, I was alert and very smart right then. The math problems were fairly whipping through my brain. Inside the convenience store I found my cup of coffee and my orange juice, placed them on the counter in front of the register, and announced to the clerk, "I'm heading over the mountains!"

The clerk stared at me. "What're you, crazy?"

I paid him no mind. He was a bit pudgy and sallow-looking, as are many graveyard-shift convenience store clerks, probably a video game enthusiast. He didn't strike me as the type to be ambitious and a go-getter, about to be lauded as a hero by his wife. Tsk, tsk, I thought. And pshaw.

And now a few moments for practical matters:

When driving across the mountains at night on a two-lane highway, it is impossible to go faster than thirty-five miles an hour. This is a fact. Try it, you'll see. Especially on Highway 88, the highway I chose. And I sense that several of you already have your hands up. Couldn't I, you ask, have driven north twenty-five miles to Reno, and there caught Interstate 80, a four-lane freeway, and crossed the mountains via that route where speeds of sixty and seventy miles an hour are possible?

Of course not.

There are two reasons for this, both so basic that to even mention them seems a waste of time and effort. The first reason is that I wanted to go home, and home was south and west of where I was.

The second reason is that I am a man. If a man needs to go south and west, it is impossible for him to even consider driving north. In fact, if a man attempts to drive north when he wants to go ultimately south and west, his head will explode. This is a simple truth. Ask any wife. She will confirm it.

So I chose Highway 88, which climbs into the mountains just south of Carson City, heading in the proper direction, a winding, two-lane highway. A winding, narrow, two-lane highway.

Going in the proper direction.

Man, it was dark out there. My headlights were yellowish and anemic, and seemed to dwindle away into the blackness, and except for the ten or twelve deer I almost hit as they streaked past, I could hardly see anything. I drank the coffee. Thirty minutes later, as instructed, I drank the orange juice. It did not give me the hour and a half of sharp focus I'd been promised. I think I got twenty minutes out of it. I cranked down my window and let the cold air blow on me. I sang. Loudly. I dug around in the glove box for a CD to play, but the only one I could find was Zig Ziglar giving a motivational speech to an Amway Convention in Des Moines in 1977. Zig was a great speaker, but after the third or fourth time through he started to lose me. I did learn how to answer objections and lead my customer toward the close of the sale, should such a need arise.

The idea that I'd made a mistake came gradually to me. I had hoped for a moon to throw some light on the road, but no such luck. In a little while it began to rain. I hunched forward over the steering wheel, staring out past the whipping wiper blades. I was up in the trees now, trees, trees, trees, branches hanging over the road, swaying mournfully in the wind, waving me back, warning of unseen perils hiding in the darkness ahead, along with more deer. My fingers ached from their death grip on the wheel. It occurred to me that the tobacco smoke swirling through my motel room hadn't been that bad, really, and maybe I could have toughed it out and eventually fallen back to sleep, and come away with only a couple of small tumors. I realized I could no longer remember the first line of Roger Miller's "Dang Me." I hummed it over and over again, thinking it would come back to me. It didn't. This was almost as bothersome as the weather.

The wind rose up behind the rain, great roaring gusts that caused the car to shudder and skitter sideways on the road. The car I drove was a small one, chosen for speed and economy, but I wished now I had brought something a little heavier, something more substantial—a Hummer, perhaps, or a Sherman tank. The wind sent waves of water slapping against the windows, reminding me of movies I'd seen about storms at sea, which made me think of shipwrecks. That didn't help. My shoulders knotted up and tried to draw together behind my ears. Though the wiper blades worked valiantly, visibility was washed down to fractions of a second, and my speed slowed to a breathtaking twelve miles an hour. Even that seemed reckless.

And in the midst of all this craziness, I suddenly, very badly, wanted to sleep.

My eyes began to ache, and burn, and feel brittle at the edges, begging to close just for a second, that's all, a couple of seconds to rest. Just for a second, maybe two little seconds, it wouldn't take long, there's not much of a curve coming up, it's pretty straight along here, or I bet it would be if I could see it, just keep a little to the right of the white line in the middle as soon as I can catch sight of it, hold steady and blink for a good long blink. Not closing my eyes, really, just doing some slow blinking.

Somewhere around four o'clock I pulled to the side of the road, got out and ran around the car three times. Then, drenched, I climbed back in, a fraction more alert now with cold water dripping out of my hair and into my face, and set off again. I sang some more. I don't remember what I sang, and it's possible no real songs came out of my mouth, just noises, noises for the sake of noise to keep me between the white lines, to keep me just this side of craziness.

I thought, it will start getting light pretty soon. . . Any minute now. It's *got* to.

The log I was swimming towards was Jackson, California, a historic little town nestled in the foothills of the Gold Country. Highway 88 runs directly into it, and this would be my point of salvation, the first outpost of civilization, where I would find gas stations, and restaurants with coffee, and electric lights, and houses with people in them. It was out there somewhere, calling to me, flashing like a beacon in my head. I knew there were highway signs along the road telling how far it was to Jackson, and I kept watching for them. Yearning for them. Desperately. But someone— some bad person—had run ahead of me and plucked up all the signs and hidden them, just to spite me. I'd been over this route before, many times, and knew there were signs. I'd seen them. Now they were gone. I didn't know who this scoundrel was, this villain who had stolen them, but I vowed to find him, and kill him. I would do this as soon as I got to Jackson, and had more coffee and orange juice.

About five AM I finally gave it up. The town I was looking for had been moved. Someone had picked it up, just like the highway signs, and scooted it another hundred miles farther west, just to foil me, and now Jackson, California was teetering at the edge of a bluff above the Pacific Ocean, possibly having shoved Monterey aside. I began looking for a wide spot alongside the highway, someplace I could pull off and lay back in the seat for a few minutes. Because I wasn't going to make it. The night was endless. Not only were my eyes drooping, but my head was drooping, and my arms and everything else even remotely droopable. Even my toes felt drooped, and that, I believe, is saying something.

I finally found what seemed a likely spot. Under some trees, of course. That's one thing they had plenty of in this part of the country. No road signs, but plenty of trees. I pulled off, cut the engine, lowered my seat into a semi-reclining position, and closed my eyes. I'd sleep for an hour. That would revive me.

The wind had calmed, but the rain was socked in, a steady, drumbeat downpour, hammering the roof. I lay there and listened to it, waiting for sleep to come and bludgeon me into oblivion. Ready for sleep, expecting it, anxious for it. Thirty minutes later I was still listening.

I discovered that it's just as hard to fall asleep in a car in the rain as it is to stay awake in one.

It struck me that this was a deep thought. Ironic, yes, but a grim sort of irony, without humor—and so profound that it bordered on philosophical truth, perhaps approaching a hitherto unknown Universal Law, something that needed to be preserved, and studied, and pondered, and debated in Universities and Think Tanks and sales yard coffee shops everywhere, and I vowed right then I would survive this ordeal and carry on, just so I could write it down and present it, polished and gleaming, to the world (which I have done, and you're welcome).

Then, after a while, I quit thinking about that. The first line of Roger Miller's "Dang Me" started playing again in my head, over and over. I remembered it now:

> *"I'm just settin' here, getting ideas*
> *Ain't nothing but a fool would live like this. . ."*

Someone tapped on my window. I jerked awake. It was still raining, but daylight at last, a thin, gray, wet daylight. A face peered in at me from a hooded sweatshirt. Under the hood was a ball cap, and under the cap was a snarl of long black hair streaked with gray, and under the hair was a big red nose and a pair of bloodshot eyes. He tapped on the window again.

I sat up and looked around. A battered blue pickup was parked alongside, idling, the smoke and steam from its exhaust curling up around it through the rain. I cranked my window down a couple of inches.

"You okay, buddy?" the guy asked. "Everything all right?"

"I'm fine, yes," I said. At least I think that's what I said. From the way he frowned at me it may have come out a bit garbled.

"What are you doing out here?"

"I just pulled over for a few minutes to rest my eyes."

"You're in my driveway. Why are you resting your eyes in my driveway?"

I sat up straighter, shook my head to clear it, and told him that I had just driven all night through the mountains from Carson City.

He blinked at me. "What're you, crazy?"

I apologized, and explained that it had been dark when I pulled over, and I'd had no way to tell this was a driveway. He pointed at a mailbox, and a sign over the mailbox, both directly in front of my car, where the headlights would be shining if they were still on, announcing to the world this was the residence of the Mooney family, Frank and Hilda.

I nodded, gave Frank—I assumed it was Frank—a sheepish grin and a wave, and started the car. Both my legs were asleep and my back was knotted into a pretzel. My head throbbed as if I'd just awakened from a two-day drunk. Frank stood watching as I pulled away, the rain running off his glasses. He looked mystified.

Fifty feet down the road stood one of the missing highway signs:

Jackson 14

The clock on the dash read 6:30 AM. I knew there was a café somewhere up ahead. I could already smell the coffee.

The rain quit about the time I hit the San Joaquin Valley, and the skies were clear when I reached Paso Robles and turned for home. The day was warm and balmy. The storm had not reached this far south. I rolled through my gate at eleven o'clock and found my dogs basking on the dirt drive in the sun. One of them lifted his head to look at me, then let it flop back down without expressing an opinion about, or interest in, my homecoming. The other dog didn't even bother to wake up.

My wife was in the yard, fussing with her roses. She wore a large pair of gardening gloves, and wielded a trowel. She saw me. She looked puzzled. She brushed the hair from her face with the back of her wrist and spoke the words every husband has heard at least once.

"What are you doing home so soon?"

I told her about the cigarette smoke at one o'clock in the morning, and my clever decision to drive through the night so that I might come home. To her. I left out the part about the rain, and all the deer I nearly hit, and waking up in somebody's driveway, figuring those details could best be told at a later time, if not forgotten altogether. There was pride in my voice, and bravado, and a desperate, dwindling hope that I might come out of this looking a little bit like a hero.

She removed her gloves and tucked them into the back pocket of her jeans. She put her hands on her hips and stared at me.

"What're you, crazy?"

THE GHOST HUNTERS

S OME PEOPLE GO out looking for ghosts.

I saw this recently on TV, where a crew with infrared cameras stumbled around at night in an abandoned building. The idea was to record any sign or sound they could attribute to supernatural things, wisps of smoke or orbs of light or clanking chains–even a floating sheet, if one was handy. *Manifestations* were what they wanted, and they'd take anything they could get.

There were four or five of these people. They called themselves investigators, and held walkie-talkies close to their faces while fanning out to different corners of the building, which was cluttered with dust and rats and old garbage. The extremely dark and cobweb-filled basement was of particular interest, as if ectoplasm had weight and would naturally sink to the lowest levels. The investigators all seemed scared they might actually see something, and spent the entire show whispering to each other over the walkie-talkies, saying things like "*Wow!*" and "*What was that?*" and "*Hoo, boy!*"

This is a bad idea on almost every level. You shouldn't go around poking up ghosts. You shouldn't shine lights on them, or rummage through the houses they allegedly inhabit, or attempt to record their spooky voices. In fact, I believe ghosts as a rule should be profoundly ignored. Keep stirring things up and no telling what might happen. On the television show the scariest thing was an empty paint can that fell off a shelf with no explanation. They stressed that. "*There was no explanation for it!*" But it could have been a rat. Nothing happened they could blame directly on a ghost, and in my book that's a good thing. I'd say they got off lucky.

It's not just television. Regular people do this, too. Old hotels seem to be a target for this kind of foolishness. I like historic buildings in historic locales, so I often stay in old hotels, but I don't go there looking for ghosts. They all seem to have one, a dead miner in the cellar, a maid who fell down the stairs in 1897, a spectral child spotted near the elevator, or some woman dressed all in white, red, or black, pick whatever color you like. The third floor of the Mizpah Hotel in Tonopah, Nevada, is supposedly haunted. Like many a hotel in many an old mining town, a harlot got shot or stabbed or strangled up there, and she's decided the best way to get even is to float around and scare people. They call her the Lady in Red, and the front desk is flooded with requests from people who want to stay in the room where she died, and can hardly wait for her to show up and do her thing, whatever that may be. Stories range from a hazy figure glimpsed in the hall, to an old crone who actually talks to you, and urges you to jump out the window. Strange things are said to happen on the third floor even if you're not staying in her actual room. The elevator on the way up gets icy cold. You'll discover your shaving kit has been moved under the bed next to your shoes, or the clock radio will go off at three in the morning, or the toilet will flush when there's nobody in the bathroom. I've stayed at the Mizpah several times, and the first thing I always do is ask them not to put me on the haunted floor, and when I get into my room I unplug the clock radio, just in case.

I'm not that kind of guy, anyway. Never have been. I've never claimed to have a direct channel to the other side, never attended seances or hung around mediums or swamis, or even played with a Ouija board, except that one time with my cousin when I was nine when he kept shoving that platter thing around so it spelled out dirty words. I've never experienced dreams where dead relatives show up and talk to me, never seen or heard omens or signs, nothing. And never wanted to.

Once, years ago, my wife and I found ourselves at the Jeffery Hotel in Coulterville, a tiny village in California's Gold Country. The Jeffery brags that it's the oldest continuously operated hotel in California, one of at least a dozen establishments here and there claiming the same honor. Built in 1852, it's a classic old west place, with a shady ramada and huge wisteria bushes twisting and climbing all the way to the second story. It was off-season, and the desk clerk said he'd do us a favor and put us in Teddy Roosevelt's room on the third floor. Apparently, Teddy came through on his way to Yosemite in 1903 and, as tradition holds, anytime a President stays in a hotel, that room is forever after named for him.

There was only one bathroom on the third floor, a community affair down the hall—quite a ways down the hall, as it turned out. At bedtime I trundled down there to brush my teeth, and when I stepped back into the hall I was suddenly struck with a case of the willies ("willies" is an expression, not a technical term. The technical term is "spooked.") There were no other guests on this floor, just my wife and me, and I realized that in this dark hallway I was now a target for any stray specter that might be hanging around, looking for the chance to scare people. I didn't believe in specters, of course, but neither did I want my lack of belief to be tested–at least not right then. I find that the strength of my convictions in such matters will weaken in direct proportion to the eeriness of my surroundings. I did the brave thing, which was to stare at my feet all the way back to the room, a trek that seemed to take forever. If there was a wispy, shimmering apparition floating anywhere in front of me, I didn't want to see it, so I just refused to look. I did not cover my eyes, though. That would have been cowardly.

My wife was in bed, reading, when I got back. She glanced up from her book.

"What happened to you? You look spooked."

"Just a case of the willies," I replied.

"A what?"

"Never mind."

I don't want to see that stuff. I don't want to have anything to do with any of it, and I never have.

I should preface this next part of the tale by admitting that I still use a flip phone. That's right, yes, a flip phone: one of those plastic gizmos with the tiny screen dating from somewhere just this side of the Jurassic Age. I realize I'll lose some of you right here, that both my credibility and relevancy will have vanished at such a mind-boggling confession, and you may feel the need to back away, as if having walked in on something delicate and embarrassing. No matter. Flee if you must. I figured out long ago I'd never be clever enough, or patient enough, to learn to use a smart phone. More shocking still, even with my flip phone I do not text.

I can hear your gasps of amazement.

My thumbs are too clumsy, and I don't want to mess with it. The texting option on my phone plan lies dormant, and dusty, and covered with cobwebs, like that abandoned building on the first page. There it is. Deal with it.

A number of years ago I was booked to perform for a guest ranch north of Tucson. The place was built back in the thirties, the hey-day of guest ranches, all adobe walls and tile roofs and decorative cacti and hitching rails everywhere. It was rumored to have been owned at one point by the Mafia, oddly enough a favorite place for the wise guys to hide out when they weren't busy murdering people and hijacking trucks and running numbers and so forth. It's impossible to know if they buried any of their victims about the property, nor do I recall hearing stories claiming they had. But after my visit there I wondered about it. I still do.

They put me in a guest cabin. It was nice enough, though you could see the age in the cracked plaster and worn floor tiles and the weary, seat-sprung armchair. I've certainly slept in worse places in my career, places I thought were not only sad but vaguely dangerous. This wasn't one of those. It was tired, but comfortable. I proceeded to the dining hall, where the stage was set up, did my show for about a hundred patrons, had a grand time and eventually returned to the cabin and climbed into bed.

And I hadn't been drinking, either. Not a drop. I feel the need to tell you that up front. I might feel the need to repeat it later, so forgive me if that happens.

At 3:15 AM, I was launched rudely from bed when my innocent little flip phone began making a huge racket, an obnoxious, brattling sound I'd never heard it make before, a sound it continued to make during the stumbling and fumbling and toe-stubbing and cursing I did, trying to wake up and remember who and where I was, and determine through which window the freight train was coming.

I found the light switch, then the dresser where my phone was bouncing around. I picked it up to discover I'd just received an Amber Alert. Somebody had snatched his or her child and was speeding away on Interstate 10, and we should all be on the lookout. I'd never seen one of those alerts, and didn't even know my phone could get one, or that they could be so loud. I felt sorely disappointed in my fellow man for choosing the middle of the night to commit these crimes.

I turned the phone off, dropped it back onto the dresser, gave it a "*Hmmph*!" and slogged into the bathroom to wash my face. My heart was pounding in my ears, and I was very much, resentfully, awake. I had no illusion of getting back to sleep anytime soon, but slid between the sheets and switched off the light to give it a try.

I lay there for no more than a minute. Really. Then I heard footsteps on the floor—my floor, right *there*—coming across the room.

And somebody laid down on the bed. Next to me.

I will repeat that. It bears repeating. *Somebody laid down on the bed next to me.*

What little hair I had left on my head stood straight up in the air. My eyes flipped open. Wide open. The room was dark as a coal mine. My heart, which had finally ticked down to a normal level, ramped right back up again. I didn't want to do it, I really, *really* didn't want to do it, but reached over to touch the covers beside me, fully expecting that somebody—or oh my God some *thing*—would be cuddled up there, and what would I do then? I hoped I wouldn't scream like a little girl, but I wasn't ruling it out.

Of course, there was nothing.

I would describe my relief for you, except I wasn't all that relieved.

I flicked on the bedside lamp and sat up against the pillows and stared out into the room for a long time. Had there been a television I would have turned it on and cranked up the volume, because everybody knows TV scares ghosts away. Or at least I think I heard that once, a long time ago. With my luck one of those paranormal shows would have come on, and tilted me completely over the edge.

Eventually I slept. I woke in the morning and played it back in my head, hoping it would all seem silly, something I could shrug off as a ripple of imagination.

I couldn't make that work. I still can't.

I won't try to explain what I experienced, because I have no idea. Nothing like it had happened before, and nothing like it has happened since. I hope it stays that way. I have difficulty accepting the fact that some people are eager to have such experiences, and will go out looking for them. On purpose.

As I said before, I think this is a bad idea on almost every level.

I also think those people are crazy.

HOW TO WRITE SONGS

I HAVE ON my desk here a letter sent by Mr. Roscoe Dimmler from Squirrel Foot, Idaho. It appears that Mr. Dimmler lives in a sheep camp up there in the flat part of the state. It's difficult to make out just what he wants, as the letter looks as if it were scrawled with a sharp stick dipped in charcoal, but in the lines I can read he's asking about how songs get written, and in particular how I go about writing mine.

He says:

> *"Dear Mister Stamler, cud you tell me how you rite yer songs. I have seed you many times and herd you, and I think if you can do it probly anybody can."*

The rest of the letter drifts off into a description of how many sheep he runs on his place, and some trouble he's having with a pesky neighbor. After that it gets smeary and unreadable. As I, proudly, know nothing about sheep, and have never met his neighbor, I can't help him with those issues, so I will limit myself to his question about songwriting—though I know nothing about that, either.

I wish I did know. I pretend that I do, but that's just empty posturing, easily seen through. I've written and recorded a bunch of them, somewhere around a hundred, I would guess, but that doesn't mean I know how to do it.

There is a story that Irving Berlin, even in his nineties, would write a song every night before going to bed. Every night. A whole song. Every goddamn night. I imagine him there, sitting at his little desk with a pencil, lamplight shining off his old bald head, humming and scribbling, humming and scribbling. Churning out these glittering lyrical jewels as easily as swatting a fly, and I kind of hate him for it. It seems wrong to hate the man who wrote "White Christmas," something you might even go to hell for, but I can't help myself. Irving wasn't all that great as a musician, by the way. Allow me to point that out with only a smidgen of snarkiness. He played piano, but just barely. He could play in only one key—I think it was B-flat—and yet there he sat, every night, popping out a finished song before shuffling down the hall to brush his teeth. If he still had any. I've heard no stories about his teeth, but that's not important. Even letting him have a weekend off every now and again, that's still over three hundred songs a year, just in the evenings, let alone what he might accomplish during daylight hours. Such a massive output almost shames me. I'm lucky if I get ten or fifteen songs in a whole year, and some years it's as few as five or six.

The nerve of the guy. I mean, really.

Diane Warren, who has written, I believe, a gazillion songs, most of them hits, and won Grammys and Tonys and Emmys and every other award ever dreamed up, says that she works at songwriting twelve hours a day, every day. She has a room she works in, like a little nest, and she claims it's never been cleaned. That's a bit scary, but not as scary as working for twelve hours, no matter what room you find yourself in. I can't think of anything I'm capable of doing for that long. Once in a while I can run a weed eater for two or three hours, but then I have to stop and drink a Fresca. I've never met Ms. Warren, and while I'm sure she's a very nice lady and I like some of her songs, twelve hours of anything is too much, I don't care what it is. Twelve hours of trying to write a song will just make you nuts.

Writers like Irving and Diane have their tried and true methods, their routines. It's called *process*. Writers talk about their process a lot. It's what writers do, often instead of actually writing something, when they're not being petty and resentful of other writer's successes. They fixate on it, and worry about it, and obsess over it, and brag to their friends how faithful they are to the process, how well it works for them–and fret and fume when the process stops working for them, and must tinker with it and bang on it until the process starts working again. It consumes writers, much the way our medical conditions and digestion consume us when they don't work properly. You have to trust the process, they say.

The word *process* indicates a series of actions, all pointed toward a specific goal. To even write a sentence like that makes me tired, and I want to find a dark room somewhere and lie down. I don't seem to have a process.

I have a goal, but no specific actions—not even one, let alone a series of them. What I do is sit around and hope a song arrives sooner or later, and you can't call that a process because it's too gradual. Almost glacial. At the end of the week I find I've written a total of two lines, neither of which seems to belong to the same song.

All that being said, for those who insist on learning the craft, and sowing discord and tension into your family life, along with financial uncertainty and general depression, here are a few tips I've picked up over the years, tricks of the trade I'm happy to pass along:

Always begin your song with "Well..." as in, "*Well*, here I sit," or, "*Well*, I ain't never," or, "*Well*, she was a large woman..." It's effective if you can drag it out for several measures, and even more effective if you shout it—the louder the better. This is the equivalent of tapping your baton against the lectern, or clearing your throat, or throwing something, a way to capture your audience's attention and let them know they're about to have a song inflicted upon them. If you can't get their attention they'll never stop chatting and ordering drinks and smoking cigarettes, and you'll have to abandon your dream of a life behind the footlights and go back to your dreary job in the toy factory.

Long, smooth vowels are preferred, as opposed to short, sputtery ones. Avoid consonants, if at all possible. Never use words with the letter K in them, or P. "Oooh," is a fine choice for a vowel, the favorite of many songwriters, and the longer you stretch it out the finer it is. Some songs have nothing but "oooh" in them, though I don't advise going down that road. It grows tedious and people stop listening, or get the feeling they've stumbled into a meditation class. "Oh" is also a good vowel, and can be used interchangeably with "well" to begin a song, as in, "Oh, my my," and, "Oh, say can you see." "Ah," however, is not recommended, as it makes people think there is a doctor with a wooden stick looking at your tonsils.

Use the word "baby" every chance you get. Do not hesitate. Throw it in there willy-nilly, like seasoning in a meatloaf. It can't be used too often—in fact, every hit song that ever rocketed up the charts contains the word "baby," as in, "Baby, I miss you," and, "Baby, come home," and, "Baby, don't take the Buick." Combine it with one of the longer vowels and you now have the recipe for a million seller, and can start thinking about paving the driveway. "Oooh, baby," and "Oh, baby," are timeless lines that echo throughout history. Elizabethan minstrels and troubadours used them, Druids chanted them under the trees, Australian aborigines employed them in their ceremonies, and I believe they can even be found in the Talmud.

It's a good idea to come up with a melody for your song people can hum, a catchy tune that gets into their heads and stays there for days and drives them crazy, like "The Flintstones," or, "Gilligan's Island." The official songwriting term for such a melody is *ear worm*, and an ear worm is always a good thing to have. Make sure you get one. I don't know how. If you can cobble together a rousing chorus that everyone wants to sing along with, that's another big plus, as long as you avoid making it a singing-in-the-round chorus, such as "Frere Jacques," or, "Row, Row Your Boat." This would be a mistake. Round singing has been declared illegal in every nation of the world, except France. They still like it over there, but they also like to eat snails and horse meat.

I'll bring this discussion to a close with a few frequently asked questions:

Q

What comes first, the words or the music?

A

Yes.

Q

I've written a song. What do I do now?

A

I have no idea. Be happy about it, I guess. Some people keep them in a drawer.

Q

What's the proper way to pitch a song?

A

I've found the best way to pitch one is to make sure it's wadded up into a very tight ball. That way it won't come uncrumpled and lose velocity on the way to the trash can.

Q

Do you have a list of publishers looking for material?

A

I suppose there are publishers out there looking for new songs, but they certainly haven't been looking for mine. Maybe you'll have better luck.

Q

How do I get my songs to Garth Brooks or Snoop Dog?

A

I don't have a clue.

Q

Should I get an agent?

A

This is not a "should" question. It's a "can you?" question, and the answer is no. Agents are interested in making money, and as a species they gave up on songwriters early in the last century.

Q

How do I get a record contract?

A

The Columbia Record Company used to have a deal where you paid full price for the first album and got the second one for a penny. You might call them and see if they're still offering that.

I hope all of this has been of some help. My plan is to stick it into an envelope and send it to Mr. Dimmler and his sheep up there in Idaho, and hope it satisfies them. If any of you have further questions, I suggest they be sent to the estate of Irving Berlin. Or, if you can find an address for Diane Warren, perhaps she can help you. Personally, I intend to get out of this songwriting racket and start playing clawhammer banjo instead. It's more socially acceptable.

GROUCH, MYRT AND THE TV NEWS

G ROUCH WAS A big, raw-boned paint horse. We kept him back in
the arena pasture, away from the dude ranch guests, because guests
are always reaching through a fence, trying to pet something, and Grouch
would bite them. He was a good using horse once you climbed on his
back. You could rope off him, or doctor cattle out in the open, anything
you needed to do, but he wasn't a pet. He didn't like being fussed at or
fussed over, and he'd nip at anyone who tried. He liked to bite other
horses as well, and would charge them and spin around to kick with both
barrels, pretty much an aggressive jerk, so we kept him back there by himself.

I'm telling about Grouch first, because this whole thing is his fault.
And Sharkey Tatum's fault, too, of course—him and those damn mustangs.

At the time I was working at a very shiny guest ranch located in a
painfully scenic valley along California's Central Coast. We'll call it the
Alamitos Ranch. That wasn't its name, but close enough. I was, God help
me, a dude wrangler, one of eight on the crew, and before you scoff, bear
in mind it was the only ranch job I ever had that offered a 401K and a
dental plan. They took care of you at the Alamitos.

We'll get back to Grouch in a minute, but first we have to get past
Myrt, the petting zoo lady, and Mr. Looten, the general manager. The two
of them are having a conversation just outside the tack room gate, which is
dangerously close to the barn for Mr. Looten. He hardly ever comes down
here. He's that tall, buttoned-down man with the eyeglasses and thinning
hair and worried look. He spends most of his time in the office, or hovering around the pool or restaurant or guest cottages, the parts of the ranch
that are get mowed and swept and dusted and polished on a regular basis.

He doesn't like it down here where the animals are, and by animals I mean horses *and* horse wranglers. The wranglers worry him, and maybe scare him a little. Even when a group of us trundle over to the employee dining room for lunch, stepping on the grass and everything—possibly coming into contact with *guests*!—it bothers him. He feels, I'm certain, we should be kept at the barn during meal times, where they can just throw hay at us, or raw meat, or whatever it is we eat. Things get dirty at the barn, and there are flies, and horse manure, and sweaty saddle blankets and God knows what else. It's best if everything down here stays down here, where it belongs.

Myrt says, "This is important, babe."

Myrt is the gray-haired woman in her seventies next to him, the one who looks like she was twisted together out of pipe cleaners and shoe leather. She runs the ranch petting zoo, where guests can drag their small children and give them the opportunity to touch a goat, or a duck, or even a pot-bellied pig, if they're brave enough. The petting zoo is another worrisome spot for Mr. Looten. He was vaguely against it from the get-go, and still seems mystified at how popular it's become.

"No, Myrt," he says. "No interviews on ranch property. Mr. Tatum has already called the front desk three times complaining about you. He's threatening to sue. The ranch can't be involved."

"You don't know what he's up to over there."

"It doesn't matter. We can't be associated in any way."

"But the TV people phoned me this morning. From Santa Barbara."

"No, Myrt."

"Those sweet horses are being starved to death, babe. Starved!"

"I appreciate your passion. I do. You can be interviewed all you want, so long as it's off property. But not here. Understood?"

You're probably wondering how I managed to hear all this. I wasn't lurking in the shadows, eavesdropping. Well, all right, I *was* eavesdropping, but not on purpose. I'm sitting in the sign-up shack next to the gate, the generic cowboy in the silver-belly hat and Carhart coat, approaching middle age, mustache already going gray, attitude veering a little more toward cranky with each passing year. I'm stuck out here, filling in for Donny, who's down with a cold or some sort of respiratory crud. I rarely pull such duty, and, when I do, perform it grudgingly, but I'd drawn the short straw this morning and being only eight or ten feet away I can't help but hear the whole conversation.

After Mr. Looten headed back toward the office, Myrt came over and leaned on the wooden counter and glared at me.

"I don't think he can do that, babe," she said.

She called everyone "babe," no matter if you were male or female, or if she knew you, or didn't. It saved her from having to remember names.

"Can't do what?" I asked.

"Keep the TV people from talking to me."

"What do they want to talk to you for?"

"On account of that damn Sharkey Tatum, that's what for," she said, jabbing a finger at me. "I took pictures of those horses, and I sent them to the newspapers to show how he's mistreating them, the poor little darlings. Now the TV news is going to get hold of it and pretty soon the whole world's going to see. He'll be sorry then, by God. Sharkey Tatum will be one sorry son of a gun."

Even though I knew better than to get sucked into this, I said, "Them horses just come off the desert, Myrt. They haven't been here but two weeks. You ought to give them a chance to bounce back and put on a little weight."

"They'll never put on weight with that piddling haystack he's got over there. You should see it, I'd bet there's not a ton of hay on the whole place, and all those mustangs wandering around with their ribs showing and burrs in their tails."

"How do you know what his haystack looks like?"

"I been over there, prowling around. Taking pictures."

"I think they call that trespassing, Myrt. No wonder Sharkey complained. Did he catch you out there?"

"He never had to catch me. I walked right up to him and told him what I thought of him. Right there in his own yard with all those dogs he has slinking around. Sometimes you just have to do what you have to do, babe."

"Oh, my."

"Listen. Speaking of breaking the law, if Mr. L won't let me talk to those TV people, isn't that taking away from my free speech? Isn't that against the law, too?"

"He never said you couldn't talk to them. He just said you couldn't talk to them here. It makes it look like the whole ranch is agreeing with you."

"Well, they should agree with me. And they would, too, if they'd seen those sweet little horses and how skinny they are. I'll just have to find someplace else to do my interview."

The situation over which Myrt was all a-flutter was what folks in the valley were calling "The Sharkey Tatum Mess." This previous winter, in Nevada, the US Government had gathered up hundreds of feral mustangs from a piece of contested BLM ground way out on the desert. Once they had these horses they didn't know what to do with them, and somehow Sharkey Tatum, local rancher, serial bridegroom and all-around rogue, wound up with two dozen of them. No one could explain why. Sharkey's ranch was along the river, not a big place, but he ran a few cows down there among the willow bushes and cottonwoods, got married and divorced about every two years—it seemed like it, anyway—and raised cow dogs, just a slew of them, once in a while winding up with one or two that would work pretty well, but not very often. The sudden appearance of a bunch of mustangs was a surprise. The best guess was some sort of mysterious back-room government contract, where Uncle Sam paid a stipend, per head, to house and feed them.

They arrived looking exactly the way you'd expect them to look, wild horses that had been rounded up with obnoxiously loud helicopters and four-wheelers, kept in BLM corrals a couple of weeks then shipped in cattle trucks four or five hundred miles: bony-hipped, gaunted and crazy-eyed, with hair knots and stickers and dried weeds in their manes and tails.

Myrt wasn't the only one up in arms. There'd already been an anonymous editorial in the local paper where the writer said nasty things about Sharkey's motives and personal hygiene, and a committee had formed to organize a town hall meeting where they could talk about it, and whip themselves into a frenzy and hand out pitchforks and torches, and all this in little more than a week. It's amazing how quickly a crusade can get rolling. According to these people the reasons the mustangs looked so poor was because Sharkey wasn't feeding them, or wasn't feeding them enough, or wasn't feeding them the right things. And doing it on purpose, too—a nasty man who in reality hated horses and brought them here at great expense just so he could be mean to them. And if the activists had their way, those poor sweet horses would be taken from Sharkey and given to nicer people, kinder, gentler folks who really cared about animals, who would pet them, and braid ribbons into their tails, and give them names. Cute names. Sharkey, on the other hand, should be executed by a firing squad, or put into a smelly dungeon for a hundred years. Or both. And tortured, too, of course.

I wondered how happy the other crusaders were going to be when they discovered Myrt had been singled out as a television spokesperson. Surely they'd prefer some frumpy guy in a sports coat and tie who could speak coherently and politely, a lawyer perhaps, someone who could lay out their complaints and concerns, and answer questions without getting angry, and even have a witty back-and-forth with the TV newsperson if the opportunity presented. Someone with tact. Myrt had all the tact of a brick through your living room window.

I don't know who stuck Old Paint in the pasture with Grouch. He may have been out there a while; I don't remember. Maybe Kate or Lisa or one of the other girls suggested to the head wrangler that having two paint horses in the same pasture would make a pretty picture, or perhaps Old Paint had been turned out with some piffling injury. I'm not blaming anybody. It was nobody's fault, except Grouch's.

Every dude ranch since the dawn of time has had a horse in their string called Old Paint. There must be a law written down somewhere that requires it, and I'd bet that every one of them was the same kind of horse. Our Old Paint was a stout, pie-bald gentleman with one blue eye. You've met him before. An old campaigner, he never caused a problem on the trail, never put a foot wrong in the arena, never did anything he wasn't supposed to do. Just a good, all around generic horse, who deserved better.

I remember it being the next day, but in my head I have the habit of compressing events into usable timelines, so it may have been as much as a week after my talk with Myrt. No matter. It was morning. On my way to the ranch I swung by Hamley's Corner Liquor Store and Quikstop for a tin of Copenhagen and a cup of coffee. I often stopped for coffee there, because it saved me from drinking the coffee we had in the tack room.

Donny assembled that coffee every morning in an ancient green 50-cup pot, and every morning it was the same evil, nasty stuff as the morning before. There was no earthly reason for coffee to taste that bad, unless you made it with stagnant pond water and metal shavings.

The Santa Barbara news van was already in the Quikstop parking lot when I pulled in, one of those big white ones with the collapsible antenna on top and *Channel 3 Eyewitness News* emblazoned across the side in bright red and blue. A thin guy in a white shirt, probably one of the techs, came out of the store balancing a cardboard carrier full of white Styrofoam cups and a paper sack which I guessed had donuts in it. He went to the van and thumped on the side with his elbow. The door slid open and he handed in the cups.

And, you know, strangely enough I never made the connection. I saw the van, recognized it for what it was, and said to myself, *Huh! I wonder what's going on.* But then I've always been notoriously knot-headed in the mornings, so I guess it wasn't all that strange. I proceeded inside, got my own coffee, and when I came out again the van was gone and I didn't think about it anymore.

Okay. So now we get to the hard part.

I'm driving my truck today, an older truck with some rusty places on it, and I've received strong suggestions that having such a vehicle parked in the front lot among the BMWs and Mercedes and shiny new SUVs doesn't make the right statement, and perhaps my truck would be happier parked out back, between the arena and the pipe pens, where we keep a dead tractor and a broken spring harrow and some bent-up Powder River panels and other old worn-out stuff. So I drive past the main entrance of the ranch to the back gate and come in that way. The Geezer Gate, we call it.

The instant I roll to a stop I can see that something is wrong.

There are wranglers clustered at the gate leading into the arena pasture, Ray and Lisa and Kate, and even old Donny, with his mousy whiskers and crumpled straw hat. I know there's a good-sized ride scheduled for this morning, and these wranglers would normally be saddling a bunch of horses and not hanging around out here. Then I spot Grouch, prancing along the back fence line with his tail in the air like an Arabian stallion in a show ring.

This is odd. Grouch can be snorty, and often is, but you never see him prance. I climb out of the truck and walk over—and that's when I see Old Paint standing in the middle of the pasture. Standing on three legs.

Oh, hell.

There is a deep, sinking sensation that happens when you walk up on a serious horse injury, a dark feeling that grabs hold and twists your insides, and you are instantly anguished and scared and angry all at the same time. You feel your heart beating in your ears. It only takes one glance to recognize the injury as a fatal one, because it's all right there, laid out for you and no questions.

"What happened?" I ask, because that's what you do, even though what happened is grimly, terribly obvious. And now here comes Mark, carrying a rifle in the crook of his arm.

Lisa looks at me with despair in her eyes. She's a tall, sun-burned girl in her thirties, her blond hair in a thick braid down her back. "Grouch did it," she says.

Mark is the assistant barn boss, one of the best horsemen I've ever worked with. Urgency vibrates around him like a cloud. He says to me, "Maybe you could find a tarp."

I run to the hay barn and grab a folded tarp from the pile, one of those cheap blue ones that are big enough to cover a dead horse, because that is what's coming. Before I turn back, I hear the crack of the rifle, a sound that causes my belly to turn over. It's always tragic when a horse has to be put down, tragedy enough when it's an old gummer teetering on his last legs, considerably worse when it's a horse you like and trust, a good one in the prime of his life.

We cover him with the tarp, tucking it under his head and hooves so the wind can't come up and flip it off him. It's a clean break on the right hind just above the pastern. Grouch had kicked at him, probably didn't even mean it. And accidentally connected. Just like somebody snapping a dry stick. Nothing to be done for it, except what had just been done.

Ray watched as Grouch continued to prance along the fence. "Need to stick him in a pen by himself where he can't hurt nobody else."

Mark says, "Good thing it happened back here and not in the front pasture where all the guests could see it."

This is the best we can do for the moment. Donny has already started for the barn, his shoulders hunched up around his ears and his hands jammed into his pockets. We all feel the same way, but it's time to bring in the rest of the horses and get them saddled. The new kid has called in sick with a hangover, and Sam, the head wrangler, is in a meeting with Mr. Looten, so we're short-handed. But that's normal: horses, as a general thing, always pick the most inconvenient moment to get themselves hurt or killed.

There are thirty people signed up for our 9:30 two-hour horseback adventure. That's how they have it written up in the brochure; it's not just a ride, it's an adventure, and we must accommodate them. We manage to finish saddling just as the guests start showing up at the tack room gate. They are happy and carefree, these people, many of them laughing, an attitude we all resent immensely in light of what's just happened. It's easy to project your own misery onto the rest of the population, and demand they share it with you, and be offended when it turns out they don't have a clue. It's natural to feel this way, and right and proper. How dare they.

It's almost ten o'clock before we can return to the arena pasture. I stop at the tool shed and grab a length of 3/8 chain. Mark fires up the tractor and heads for the pasture gate. I jump on behind, standing on one of the arms of the three-point hitch.

Every ranch has its bone yard, sometimes called the dead pile, an out of the way spot to drag and leave the unfortunate victims of agricultural mortality. You can't dig a hole every time a calf dies—on some places if you did that you wouldn't have time to do anything else. Our bone yard is in a side canyon across Alamitos Road, out of sight of the ranch, a tranquil place where the buzzards roost peacefully in the oak trees. It's there that Old Paint's last ride will end.

I swing down and open the gate. Mark drives through and I close it behind him, pausing to look over at Grouch, who has settled down and now stands quietly, guiltlessly, cropping grass next to the petting zoo fence just like he never broke anybody's leg. I grab the chain from the front bucket and flip the tarp open. With the chain I take a double wrap around Old Paint's hind legs and then stand waiting as Mark wheels the tractor around and backs toward me.

"Just going to drag him out?" I ask.

"Don't know what else to do."

You know how you can see something, and it doesn't get all the way to your brain? You're busy, your mind is on other things, things that are immediate and close to hand, like spooling the chain around the tractor's trailer ball and setting the hook. As I do this, I notice a van on the other side of the fence, parked out on Alamitos Road, kind of dead center to the pasture, a white van with red and blue lettering across the side, and I don't think anything about it, except *oh, there's a van.* Cars go up and down this road all the time. Maybe somebody has a flat. It's only later, after it's too late, I realize that people are standing outside the van, and one of them looks angular and leathery and gray, the way Myrt always looks. If I stop and think about it, which I don't, I might notice, as I'm sure you already have, that the big round thing on top of the van looks a great deal like a satellite antenna, and the boxy black thing one of the other people is holding looks like a camera. A news camera. A big one.

I give the thumbs up. Because at this point I am still clueless. Mark eases the clutch about halfway out and the tractor creeps forward until the slack is out of the chain. Old Paint remains where he is. Mark feathers out a bit more clutch, and gives it a bit more gas, and you can see the big rear tires grip the ground and even sink a little as the engine strains. Old Paint still stays put. This is puzzling. He's a fair-sized horse, but not that big. This is a full-grown John Deere tractor, with enough poop to yank a small building around.

Mark lets off on the gas and throws the shifter into neutral. "What's he hung on?"

I get on my hands and knees in the still-wet grass to investigate, but I already think I know. A couple decades back a former maintenance manager engineered an in-ground irrigation system for this pasture, a tangle of galvanized pipe and pop-up Rain for Rent sprinkler heads that hasn't worked in years, if it ever did. The sprinkler heads are still here, though, waiting to be tripped over, and broken off when the feed truck rolls across them, and snagged up in your spike harrow, and so on.

"I think he's caught on one of them damn sprinklers."

"Can we lift him off of it, you think?"

"Maybe."

I unwrap the chain from the trailer ball. Mark turns the tractor around and lowers the front bucket, and I coil the chain around the bucket and set the hook over the lip. Mark gently curls the bucket until the slack again pulls tight. Once more I give the thumbs up. He raises the bucket. Slowly. And up comes Old Paint.

Okay, so here's the picture: We are now hoisting this unfortunate animal into the air until he hangs, upside down, like a carcass on a butcher's hook. I cringe at using that phrase, but it is appropriate, since that's exactly how the news anchor on CNN will describe it only a few hours later, after the whole thing goes national. I believe the people at Fox News were a bit less caustic with their coverage, but they sure enjoyed running the footage, over and over and over again.

We get him off the ground, and Mark gently backs the tractor so to clear the sprinkler before laying him down again. It's then I take another look at the van. The big white van, with the TV station logo on the side. And yes, that's Myrt out there, giving her interview–off property, as instructed by Mr. Looten, but just barely. Three people stand with her, all of them looking at us, and one of them holds a microphone.

Realization is what they call it. The *oh, hell* moment.

I wave my arms at Mark. "*Down!*" I shout. "Bring him *down!*"

He can't hear me over the tractor engine and it takes a few seconds to get his attention. I hop frantically in place, wave my arms some more, then take off my hat and wave that.

"*Down! Down down down!*"

He hits the lever and Old Paint sinks back to earth. I scramble for the blue tarp and drag it back over him, then sit down on top of it all as if having suddenly decided this is the perfect spot to take a break and look out upon the morning, to look at the thin kid by the van holding the camera, the skinny kid in the white shirt I recognize as the coffee and donut guy from the Quikstop, and that is sure enough a camera, a sturdy black professional camera of the sort used by TV people to document breaking news like riots and tsunamis and political rallies and other disasters. It's pointed right at us. The lens looks just like a gun.

It's all over the news that evening, and I do mean everywhere. You probably saw it six or seven times yourself, because they ran it for a solid week: Myrt, lean and wrinkled, smoking one of her Virginia Slims and speaking in ominous, gravelly tones about people who mistreat animals, while in the background two cowboys drag a dead horse around with a tractor, apparently just for fun. The legend at the bottom of the screen announces that this is taking place at the Alamitos Guest Ranch on California's Central Coast. Some people dream of being on television and never get the opportunity; to these people I say count your blessings and go on about your life and be happy. Other say there is no such thing as bad publicity, but people who say that don't know what the hell they're talking about.

Myrt's crusade against Sharkey Tatum got lost in all the smoke and noise. At least half the local newscasts forgot to mention him at all, so great was their glee over what Mark and I were up to. Some of the national coverage included only Myrt's generic railing against animal cruelty before they zoomed in on that damned tractor. All the details concerning Sharkey and his bad hay and evil intentions and lack of human decency were edited out so that viewers could better appreciate the gratuitous irony. I don't think Myrt has forgiven us yet.

Mark and I both were summoned to Mr. Looten's office the next morning, where we attempted to explain how such a thing could happen. Mr. Looten had quit answering the phone by now, and directed Margaret on the switchboard to tell all callers that the ranch had no comment at this time, thank you very much. He sat with his elbows on the desk and his chin in his hands as we told our story, and I think he was listening to us. It was hard to tell. He didn't look at us, or at anything in particular, and his expression made me think of a hound dog who had been kicked off the porch one too many times. After a moment he got up and went to the window. Out there on the road at the end of the driveway a cluster of PETA protesters waved their cardboard signs. They'd been there all morning, since about five AM.

Mark and I sat in silence for a minute. Finally Mr. Looten said, "Just go. Please. Get out of my sight. Just go away."

THE MASON BROTHERS

I DON'T REMEMBER why we were branding on a Tuesday. It happens sometimes, but not often—usually you want to schedule your branding for the weekend, so you can get enough good help, especially up on the Mason Ranch, which is where we were. The Mason brothers always have a slew of calves to brand, I think 150 head that day, and you have to gather them first, some steep, nasty country covered with rocks and scrubby little blue-oak trees, hardly an inch of flat ground on the place. It'll wear your horse out. The reason it was Tuesday was probably just because of branding season, with everybody trying to get their calves worked at the same time. Hardly anyone keeps full-time cowboys on the payroll anymore, certainly not the Mason brothers, so you're left to rely on your neighbors, and there's only so many to go around.

There were seven of us in the branding pen, me and Glenn and Barry working ground crew, ear-marking and castrating and running the vaccination guns. On horseback we had the two Kutcher boys and Nuno Silva and another guy I don't remember his name. Charlie Mason had been pushing the calves up, ten at a time, and Herb Mason was wielding the hot iron, but at 11:30 exactly Charlie tied his horse next to the loading chute, and Herb looked at the rest of us through the dust and said, "Keep at it, boys! Marguerite will holler for lunch in a few minutes!" And the two of them scurried up the hill to the house.

Herb and Charlie are twins, seventy years old at least, both bow-legged and stiff as dried harness leather, and I don't believe I've ever seen either one of them smile. They're not identical twins. Charlie has a mustache, so you can tell them apart real easy. They're third or fourth generation on this place, have worked it all their lives and never had a job in town, except for Herb, who was in the Navy a long time ago. They live here with their daddy, Lance, who is 94 years old and was sitting in a lawn chair outside the corrals, watching.

Old Lance squinted at me through the fence and said, "What the hell they doing?"

I need to talk a little about the way brandings go, usually. The good ones, I mean. You gather your cattle, push them into the corrals and sort off the calves, and then rope and throw each one down and brand him and inject him with Four-Way vaccine, and squirt tick dope in his ears and so on, until all of them are done. This can take well into the afternoon. Then, after the work's finished, you drink beer, and barbecue steaks, and sit around and laugh and gossip about the people who aren't here, and basically have a party. That's how good brandings go.

The Mason brothers, on the other hand, do not make a party out of it. They like to break for lunch when it's lunch time, and they don't provide steaks, or beer. Lunch is some kind of stew, generally, or white bread sandwiches you have to make yourself, or pork and beans with hot dogs, the kind of stuff you might get at a homeless shelter. Then you go back out and brand the rest of the calves, and afterwards everybody just goes home, feeling a little disappointed.

But the Masons had never abandoned us a half hour before lunch. This was a new twist.

Eventually Marguerite came out on the porch and clanged the dinner bell. Marguerite is a stout Mexican lady, and I've never quite figured out if she works for the brothers as a housekeeper, or is actually married to one of them, and if so which one. She always has a sour look on her face that discourages personal inquiry. We went up and washed our hands and filed into the dining room. Marguerite had removed all the feed invoices and veterinary pamphlets and broken bridles and old copies of *Western Horseman* from the table and piled them in a corner so we'd have a place to sit down, and stacked bowls and spoons and napkins in the middle and lugged in a big vat of her chili verde. This was lunch, along with some tortillas, and even though they weren't homemade tortillas, they were pretty good.

The old man said, "Where's them boys at?"

Marguerite said, "They in there, with their thing. You know."

"No, I don't know. What the blue blazes are you talking about?"

"Every day. The same thing every day," Marguerite said. She shook her head in disapproval, then toddled off to go sit in the kitchen until we all went away again.

It was another ten minutes before Charlie and Herb reappeared, their old bald scalps gleaming pale and naked without hats to cover them. They grabbed bowls and ladled in some chili verde and sat down at the far end of the table, without saying anything to anybody except themselves. They weren't exactly whispering, but they spoke so softly you could only catch about every other word.

Lance groused, "Where'd you boys sneak off to?"

They ignored him, and dug into their lunch. I heard Charlie say, "You figger he knows?"

Herb shrugged. "I don't think so. I don't think he's the one, neither, no matter what she claims. It's a rook deal."

"He never was no good, you ask me. A no-good son of a buck, is what he is."

"You're right about that."

Lance scowled, his bird-like head craned forward. "Who's no good? Who are you talking about?" He turned and scowled at me. "Who they talking about?"

The boys ignored him, and continued to whisper and mumble at each other, as serious as church. After a few moments it began getting heated, and Charlie stabbed a finger against the table and said, "You remember, he borrowed all that money from her. You think she'll ever see a cent of it back? Like hell she will."

Lance said, "I know who you're talking about. It's that little Donny Poindexter, ain't it? I told you not to let him come around here no more."

Herb said, "No, Dad, we ain't talking about Donny Poindexter."

"Calls himself a horseshoer. He lamed up that bay horse, bigger'n hell."

"It ain't Donny Poindexter. Go on and eat your lunch. Mind your own business."

"Mind my own business? Well! I like *that*."

Barry picked up his bowl and stacked it with mine and Nuno's, and carried them into the kitchen. Barry's a walnut farmer, and a damn good cowboy to boot, and smiles all the time. He's short and kind of round, and wears a ballcap every day, even at brandings. We could hear him in there, joshing with Marguerite, and Marguerite said something back to him and even laughed, which was remarkable. Only Barry could manage that. The rest of us would be scared to even try, afraid she'd grab a meat cleaver and run us out of there. She might be stout, but I bet she could move pretty quick if she was mad enough.

Charlie ripped a tortilla in half and wiped his bowl with it and stuffed it into his mouth. He drained his coffee cup and, still chewing, said, "All right, fellers, might as well get after it. No use staying here all night." He and Herb scraped their chairs back, grabbed their hats and stomped out.

The rest of us rose and stretched and found our own hats. I'd left mine on a chair in the hallway. I went in and got it, and looked at the photographs on the wall. There was a dozen or so, hanging in cheap dime store frames, old pictures of old cowboys in 1940's clothing, sitting horseback in the corral, or posed next to old trucks and hump-backed cars, booted feet up on running boards. I thought I could pick out a young version of Lance in a few of them, staring out at me through the yellowed glass from back in the hardscrabble days.

Walking down the hill Barry caught up with Glenn and me. Smiling, as usual. He said, almost in a whisper, "It's *Days of Our Lives*."

Glenn said, "What is?"

"The soap opera. *Days of Our Lives*. Herb and Charlie are hooked on it."

Glenn stopped and started at him. "You gotta be kidding."

"You remember when Herb was laid up with that broke leg a couple years ago. That's when they got sucked into it. Marguerite says they watch it every single day. Can't bear to miss it."

"They left their own branding to go watch a TV show?"

"It's a strange old world, ain't it? I got to go help Lance. He has a tough time hobbling around out here."

At the corrals Herb was punching up the branding fire, and Nuno and the rest were tightening cinches. It was a nice day, the temperature pleasant and not a cloud in the sky—but I thought I could hear a faint whirring sound in the air. I decided it must be the cowboys in those old photographs, spinning around in their graves.

1963 DODGE STEPSIDE

THERE ARE TOWNS, they say, in Kansas and Nebraska, small, vanishing brick-fronted towns where it's possible to buy a house, right now, for about $85,000. Really. I'm serious. And if you aren't married to the idea of an intact roof and indoor plumbing, you might get one for even less—granted, out there in the heartland, where they forgot to invent hills, and the horizon goes on for weeks, and every so often tornados come after you, but these bargains exist. I haven't priced them personally, but I'm told they are there and I choose to believe it, because believing it, and convincing you to believe it, helps to make my point.

And what point might that be, you ask?

That new pickup trucks are too damn expensive.

Just go with me on this.

In 1992 my wife and I purchased a Ford F250, white in color—I think that was the only color they made back then—the first and only vehicle we ever bought new off the lot. We haggled and fretted with the sales people, spent a week's worth of sleepless nights, and changed our minds twenty-three times before making the jump. It was a traumatic purchase. You'd have thought we were mortgaging our own kidneys. After everything was totted up, the astronomical price at the bottom of the contract was $17,000. I think the National Debt at the time was only $25,000. We financed it, of course, because we were young then and still believed in hope, but even with a substantial down payment that included cash, a goat, several chickens and some costume jewelry I'd inherited from my grandfather, it was a debt we thought would never be paid off, a burden that would be passed along to our heirs, perhaps several generations hence.

I still own that truck. I still pull a stock trailer around with it. I haul feed with it. I pile stuff in the bed and drive it places and dump it out again, and then go get more stuff. It does everything trucks were meant to do, and there's not a scratch on it. A little rust, sure. That's to be expected, after almost thirty years. The heater doesn't work anymore, but that's why God invented coats and wool caps. There are lint-covered tools and old McDonalds wrappers under the seat that have been down there for fifteen years, but damn it, it's a truck. It continues to serve us well. And it's paid for.

But.

Things are beginning to fail, here and there, little pieces that wear out, or fall clean off. I lost the passenger side mirror a while back, and I still don't know where that went. One day it was just gone. I had to replace it, which proved unsettling, because the new one is shiny and gleams in the sun like polished silver, and looks jarringly out of place on such a mature truck, as though someone dragged Aunt Maude down to the piercing store and got her a nose ring. The starter has a habit of quitting me every three or four years, and I've had to change out the water pump and hoses, the alternator and the master cylinder; and three or four times a day you need to thump on the dash with the flat of your hand to get the radio to come back on. Little stuff like that.

The engine is still strong. Every two years I trundle down to the Orange Cove Auto and Smog Repair Shop for my smog inspection, and the guy there scratches his head and tells me, with wonder in his voice, that the readings are all perfect, once again. They're always perfect, and he's always amazed. My truck is the octogenarian who aces the stress test every time. And I am reassured. Still, a part of me knows I'll be driving along one of these days, and *boom*! There will come a loud explosion and, like some character in a Mack Sennett comedy, I'll find myself sitting in the middle of the highway holding nothing but a steering wheel with the rest of the truck in pieces around me. People will honk and wave as they drive past, and someone will cue the silly Laurel-and-Hardy music that always plays at the end of these scenes. Then, and only then, will it be time for a new truck.

But I've started thinking about it.

I have a regular car I use when it's time to go on tour. It's a late-model vehicle, with two sun-roofs and a GPS and countless other bells and whistles, including a radio you don't have to hit, but it doesn't possess the history or the personality of an old truck. I have it serviced at a local dealership, and I was down there the other day waiting for an oil change when

I saw, out on the street, an even more ancient pickup go limping past, a 1970s vintage, rust-pocked, wheezing and clanking, trailing an oily cloud of exhaust. Suddenly the mortality of my own truck, always at the back of my mind, rushed to center stage. Troubled and heartsick, I wandered out to the display lot, where the new trucks were lined up in shiny formation.

Gone are the days when prices were displayed on windshields in numbers a foot high, and you could see what you were up against forty feet away. Now you must get close to the vehicles, and look around for quite some time before finding the window they've taped the white piece of paper onto, and then get out your reading glasses, because the print is very small.

Trucks are different than they were in 1992. They are all built like luxury cars with truck beds attached, but none of them look like anything you'd want to stack a couple of bales of hay in. They have back seats, like sedans, and genuine imitation wood highlights on the door panels and pop-down video screens for the kids in the back, individual climate control, electronic gizmos everywhere—everything but a wet-bar, and I may have just missed that. The white paper on the window lists the options each truck possesses, and how much money each option adds to the price, options such as symphonic quality stereo speakers or all-wheel drive or a live-in butler or part-time cook. I looked at the price tag on three of these trucks, then had to find a place to sit down so I could catch my breath.

The first was $83,000. The second was $78,568.00, and the third was $86,256.37. I didn't have a clue what the thirty-seven cents was for, perhaps some of the air in one of the tires.

Stunned is a good word for the way I felt. Shocked, confused and bewildered are also good words, and certainly appropriate, but mostly I was stunned.

With the amount of money they wanted for a new truck, I could go to Kansas or Nebraska, and buy a house.

This was a strange new world, a bizarre world, one I hadn't realized existed, and for all I knew might be inhabited by evil leprechauns or flying monkeys. It made no sense.

In the world I come from, which contains no mythical creatures, people don't pay $85,000 for a pickup. If you suggested such a thing to any of the folks I grew up around, they'd have given you the same puzzled look a pig gets when you show it a pocket watch. They would not have offered you a beer, or even a cup of coffee, but would have tried to get you out of the house as quickly as possible without making a scene, because obviously you are a crazy person.

I bought the first truck I ever owned from my father, a 1963 Dodge half-ton stepside that was pretty much used up when I got it. I paid him $200 for it. I made payments, twenty bucks a month, which coincidentally was what he paid me for feeding cows and setting fence posts and stacking hay and every other chore that came up. A win-win for the old man, certainly. He was done with the truck, having recently moved up to a $400 Chevrolet, and all his ranch labor was suddenly cost-free, which, now that I think of it, nudged our relationship dangerously close to slavery.

This venerable beast had the old 225 slant-six engine, with a single-barrel carburetor and oil bath air cleaner, and the engine had been bored out and rebuilt so many times it was probably a 226 by now. It had been abandoned in the weeds and weather next to the bull pasture for at least a year, where it became home for all kinds of creatures, four-legged and eight-legged, and about three times a day you'd have to pull to the side of the road, rummage for the 7/16 end-wrench you kept in the glove box and take the fuel line loose to pluck out whatever bits of mouse fur and weeds and bug parts had been sucked off the bottom of the gas tank. It wasn't a very complicated task, a routine I figured everybody had to do, and the carburetor was fairly primitive. I think it was the same one they used on most of the lawn mowers back then. Occasionally you'd have to go in a little deeper, and disassemble the needle valve, cussing and grousing by the side of the highway as the cars whizzed past, and invariably you'd drop that little plunger dealie and have to crawl under the truck and dig around in the dirt to find it again, and wipe it down with your shirt tail before putting everything back together. Once I tweezered an entire dead grasshopper out of there. If you tried going faster than 45 miles an hour it would shake and shudder and shimmy like an 85-year-old burlesque dancer. The only fast thing about it was the speed at which it burned through re-cap tires.

I drove it through my high school years and, looking back, what's remarkable is that it wasn't remarkable. It was just a truck. Not the average truck, probably way down on the lower end of average—a C-minus, maybe—but certainly not the worst one in the school parking lot. You might have found a few shiny, late-model cars out there had you gone looking, cars owned by the snooty rich kids, but even those weren't new. In fact, I never heard of anyone in our grease-gun-and-baling-wire circle of friends and acquaintances buying a brand-new car or truck. Ever. There were rumors that some people, somewhere, did such things, but they were like Sasquatch, or a state senator, or naked girls, things you heard about and never actually saw.

The Dodge died a gradual death the year I turned eighteen. A mule kicked in the driver's side door one day and it wouldn't stay closed anymore. There was always the danger it would suddenly fly open if you took a sharp left turn. The rain gutter around the edge of the roof rusted completely through, so that the wind roared in at you, along with the rain if there was any, and made it hard to hear the radio, or get dates. Or more than one date. The engine deteriorated until finally it was using as much oil as gasoline; one day it seized up solid, never to crank over again.

After that I paid twelve hundred bucks for a blue Datsun pickup with a clunky rear end and wheel bearings that whistled like a banshee if you tried going faster than fifty-five miles an hour, one of those half-sized trucks that became popular after the fuel shortages of the mid-1970s. You could only stack about half a ton of alfalfa in the bed, eight bales tops, and you couldn't tow anything with it, but it got twenty miles a gallon and the doors would stay closed when you went around corners. The little four-banger engine blew up on me one night at two AM on the 101 freeway and I had to walk seven miles home in the dark. I bought an engine from a crow-infested junk yard on Sheridan Road and got it going again, but in my mind the truck had betrayed me and I always held a grudge. I don't think it liked me very much, either. I eventually sold it to a hippy who lived in a camper trailer out amongst the eucalyptus trees. I don't recall how much I sold it for, but since the hippy never paid me I don't suppose it matters. I do remember that he had a stringy looking girlfriend who wore long skirts and heavy boots, and that she scared me. She didn't like cowboys.

"People shouldn't ride horses," she told me. "Horses should run free."

I told her it happened that way sometimes. She and the hippy ran free themselves one night, taking the Datsun with them.

There were other trucks as the years rolled by. A shiny, red and white Chevy Luv in which my wife and I travelled all over the west, up firebreak trails and in and out of desert washes and brushy canyons, places a two-wheel drive truck wasn't supposed to go. A 1964 Ford Unibody, primer-red from nose to tail, that I'd hoped to restore and never did. It was a rattling, clattering vibrating relic with a six-cylinder engine and a sand-blasted windshield that blinded you when the sun reflected off the pocks and divots in the glass. I used it to haul hay, and drag a little two-horse trailer around, and to clear out and pack away a half acre of prickly pear cactus that had grown up against the horse pasture fence. It proved to be a work horse—again, not pretty, but functional. A tool. A good tool, which is, I think, what pickups were meant to be.

Recently I found myself in southern California, attending an annual equine event I've been associated with for several years. Orange County, which is one of the places that has transformed the truck from useful tool into an urban accessory, the way a fancy purse or an expensive pair of boots are accessories. Damn few sacks of rolled oats get carted around in truck beds down there. I was standing in the parking lot visiting with some folks I vaguely knew, making small talk, when I saw a vehicle pull into the lot from the street. I immediately lost the ability to speak, or even conjure up a coherent thought. The people I'd been talking with looked at me with sudden concern, perhaps wondering if I'd had a stroke.

Coming toward me, it's motor rumbling smoothly, the chrome of its front bumper shining in the late afternoon sun, was a brand new 1963 Dodge half-ton step side, and my old heart did a flutter and a flip. It parked, right there in front of me, and an acquaintance of mine named Eric stepped out of it and hailed me.

I did not answer him. I stumbled forward, my eyes bugging out and my jaw hanging slack. I circled the truck, twice, and then a third time, full of wonder and delight. Then and only then did I look at Eric.

"Where," I said, "did you find this?"

"Ain't it great?" he said.

It was my old truck, born anew. The paint was show-room perfect, the windshield crystal clear and free of cracks, the wood planking of the bed polished, gleaming, unscarred. The leaf springs were solid and firm, there was no sag anywhere, and those weren't re-cap tires—and holy cow, he even had the half-moon hubcaps, *all four* of them, perfect for dropping the lug nuts into when you were changing a flat tire, which I'd had to do many times. The spare tire was bolted properly to the side, where it was supposed to be, rather than laying in the bed where I'd always kept mine.

Eric told me he'd just bought it, from an outfit down there near Irvine that specialized in restoring classic trucks. He said this one just seemed to speak to him. "It's got a three-speed on the tree, can you believe it?"

"Yes," I said, "I can. I sure can."

I asked him what he paid for it—a rude question, but I just had to know. He said he'd given $22,000 for it.

Brand spanking new, in 1963, the truck had been stickered at $2400. Now, somehow, a price of nearly ten times as much did not seem out of line. Had I been carrying that much cash in my pocket I would have gladly handed it over and driven the old girl home.

Or maybe all the way to Kansas, or Nebraska.

I hear there are real estate opportunities.

TERRITORIAL WEATHER

WE WERE EATING a late breakfast when a bulletin sprang up on the television, notifying us of a tornado watch for the immediate area. This alarmed me more than just a little. Our friend Kathy stepped out the back door onto her porch and stood there for a moment, looking at the sky. She came back inside and shook her head. Shrugged. Like it was no big deal.

"It's not anywhere near us. I can tell. When they're close by I can feel the pressure fluctuations against my face."

It was early autumn and we were in Kansas. I think of Kansas people as being sensible and sober, with both feet firmly on the ground, but the idea of knowing that much about tornados seemed bizarre. And then, out of nowhere, she said, "Tornados don't bother me. What I don't get is how you live in California with all those earthquakes all the time."

Wait a minute here. I have heard Kansas people actually say "tornado season," two words which, in my opinion, should never be that close to each other. California, on the other hand, though frantic to legislate absolutely everything else, has yet to announce an official season for earthquakes. Earthquakes are rare. Years go by, even decades, between events. People sometimes forget they happen at all. Tornados are much more reliable. You can count on a half dozen of them to rip through every year, and tear up stuff. Especially mobile home parks. But no, the elusive earthquake is the bigger, more terrifying boogeyman, and gets all the bad press, and furthermore anybody who lives where an earthquake might occur must be pure bat-ass crazy.

This is an example of the logic of territorial weather.

No matter where you live, there is some sort of weather "thing" unique to your region, and it scares the dog poop out of anybody who doesn't live there. It even becomes a point of pride, a badge of honor, because for you it's just a fact of life, something you've gone through again and again, and you're used to it, and can therefore treat it with a nonchalance that leaves outsiders standing open-mouthed and amazed. Sometimes you can even get cocky about it.

"What? Ohhh. . . Now that you mention it, I guess a tornado did come through here. A little bitty one. I wasn't really paying attention."

Growing up in Montana, for us it was winter. This was our banner to wave. When winter arrives in that region it sits down hard, puts its feet up, and hangs around for a long time. I particularly remember January of 1970, when the thermometer crashed to 45 below. And, in my head, the temperature stayed right there, for weeks and weeks, never wavering, transforming life into a polar expedition and bringing time itself to a complete standstill. I'm pretty sure, realistically, it didn't happen quite that way, but that's how I remember it. I know that 45 below was seen, several times, but probably only briefly, on its way up to a high of ten below or five above, the way it always happens. But that is the art of exploiting territorial weather. You have such experiences, and at the time you shrug them off, because that's just life and you don't want to look like a weanie. Then, later, you take those experiences and inflate them, exaggerate them, adorn them with horrific details, and shrug them off again.

"Yes, every small child in Yellowstone County lost a toe that winter. But! What the hell."

In the southeast, bragging rights seem to center around hurricanes, and living through them, and these are, to my way of thinking, even more frightening than tornados. A tornado is gone in a few minutes. Hurricanes come roaring in like an alcoholic father-in-law, and stay for three or four days, picking up bank buildings and strip malls and changing their addresses by moving them from here to there, dumping entire acre feet of rain at a time, causing the ocean itself to rise from its bed and slap things silly. I am sorry, but if you hang around for more than one of these, you are out of your mind, and I can rustle up half a dozen psychiatrists to sign the papers. But people do hang around. And brag about it, after they shrug it off, and nail plywood over their windows—because that's going to be enough protection, isn't it—and barricade themselves inside with beer and potato chips and finger food, and wait these things out.

You heard me. That's right, two more words that should never be used together: weather, and barricade. If they happen in the same sentence, something in your life has gone horribly, horribly wrong. Yet, hurricane people will stand up next to tornado people, who will stand beside extreme winter people—lunatics who barricade themselves against their weather every year—and all of them will look at California and announce that an earthquake is the real deal-breaker.

"I just don't see how you live out there," they say.

THE BREAKFAST RIDE

I'VE COME HERE today to talk about the dreaded breakfast ride. This is a painful subject for me, and in bringing it up I hope to conjure a little respect and understanding, but failing either of those I will settle for pity. Anyone who's had to endure them on a regular basis knows that the very mention can cause a loss of appetite and a sense of impending doom. And when I say anyone, I'm of course talking about dude wranglers.

As an entertainment, the breakfast ride belongs almost exclusively to guest ranches. Every so often, a hunting outfitter or hapless pack station, tucked away on a nameless mountain, will flirt with the idea of putting dudes on horses, dragging them to a scenic, inconvenient spot and cooking bacon and scrambled eggs for them, trying to keep dirt out of the frying pan and pine needles from the gravy. Pack station people and outfitters as a species, however, have a low threshold of aggravation (not to mention a perpetual hangover), and after a few miserable attempts they give it up and retreat back into hiding.

At the Alamitos Ranch, where I toiled for an alarming number of years, breakfast rides tumbled along with hideous regularity. Twice a week during the off season, which was bad enough, but come summertime and Spring Break it shifted to three times a week: Tuesdays, Thursdays and Saturdays—and after a while it felt as though breakfast rides were all you ever did, you finished one and here came another, again and again, until your eyes glassed over and you no longer had the energy or the will to lift your chin off your chest.

Allow me to elaborate.

The ride I'll describe for you takes place during Spring Break, which, in olden days, was called Easter Vacation and lasted a sensible two weeks. I don't know when the change happened, or who was responsible, but someone discovered that if you left off the Easter part and called it Spring Break instead, you could stretch it out for six weeks—six solid, endless, tortuous weeks, and if I ever meet that person I intend to hurt him, and badly.

Picture yourself at the horse barn. Six AM, and still dark. The forecast is calling for—you guessed it. Rain.

It's cold enough to see your breath in the circle of light from the fly-specked bulb over the tack room door. A fire blazes in the burn barrel, wafting the gentle tang of diesel fumes across the corral. Dust hangs in the air, and now comes the rumble of hooves as Ray pushes the first fifteen horses up the alley, followed by the clang of the steel gate slamming behind them. Sam wrangled them in half an hour ago, and now the herd mills uneasily back there in the darkness of the grain pen. The horses know what's coming, and are anxious to get on with it; they jostle each other, biting, squealing.

Sam is in the catch pen, hopped up on too much caffeine and Lord knows what else, frenetic, grabbing halters from the iron hooks on the fence rail, catching horses, dragging them three at a time to the saddling pen gate. Last night he scribbled up a catch list, and it hangs there on a clipboard next to the halters, but he never looks at it. He doesn't need to. He knows which horses are going, and the people assigned to them; he can summon up the name of every guest on the ranch with the acuity of a warlock. He laughs as he works, he jokes, he barks orders, his voice harsh against the slate-cool morning. He is big and athletic, with energy crackling in the air around him like electricity. One thing he can't do is sing, but he tries anyway, croaking fragments of lyrics that only vaguely resemble actual songs.

"*I believe I can fly. . .!*"

On the wall beside the tack room door hangs a large whiteboard, and on this board is a roster of every horse in the herd. A hundred and twenty names. Beside the name of each horse is scrawled the name of its impending rider. Near the bottom a circled number shows the count for today's ride. Sixty dudes.

Sam hollers, "Happy Easter, boys and girls!"

It's too dark to see the clouds yet, but we can feel them over us, heavy and damp. Ten of us are working this morning and, just like the horses, we know what's coming. We know what to do. We've done it a million times–or it seems like a million times, anyway:

Grab a horse as Sam sends them in through the gate. You know which ones will tie and which ones will not, their personalities, their quirks, the strange little boogie-men who live in their heads. You can tie Bullwinkle with a piece of frayed kite string and set off a bomb under his feet and he won't so much as blink. Latigo can't be led to the rail at all, he'll set back at the first tug on his halter, so you must saddle him in the middle of the corral with the lead rope draped across your arm. When you do tie one up, use a quick-release manger knot—a wrap around the rail, then a loop, then pass the bite through with another loop, then snug. Katie or Lisa, or maybe the new kid who hasn't learned all the horses yet, will swoop in with brush and curry comb to clean the back where the saddle will go, and where the cinch will snug against the belly. Inspect for galls, or sore places on the way to becoming galls. Knock the worst of the crud off the rest of him and move on. It's a breakfast ride, not a horse show. White horses, flea-bit grays and paint horses will always have green blotches on them, because, prowling the feedlot last night, minds full of mischief, they found a nasty spot, some vile puddle of fresh mud and wet green manure, and happily flopped down to roll. This is done on purpose, of course.

Every horse has a number. They're listed on the whiteboard beside the names. Go ahead and take a look, though you probably don't need to: Sox is number 50 and has been forever; Apache is 63, Lucky is 46. Hurry into the tack room, grab the bridle from its numbered hook on the wall, then on to where the saddles wait on their numbered wooden racks that have been here since 1946. With the bridle hung on your left shoulder and the saddle blankets over your left arm, grab the saddle by the gullet with your right hand, and tote the whole load out to the horse. Flip the blankets onto his back, straighten them, at the same time swinging the saddle up and over in a practiced arc so the off stirrup clears. Settle the saddle into place, flip the cinch over, reach under the horse to catch the cinch coming up, slip the latigo through and up to the D-ring. Untie the lead rope and step the horse away ten or fifteen feet before drawing up the cinch. Wriggle a thumb into the corner of his mouth and offer him the bit, guide it gently into place and slip the headstall over the ears. Smooth the forelock. Reins up and over and half-hitched to the saddle horn, and you have a pony who's properly dressed and ready to receive a pilgrim. Find a spot on the back rail and tie him.

Repeat.

And repeat.

"Scout's lost a front shoe," Katie says.

Sam shouts, "Tyrell!"

"Got it!" Tyrell strides over, collects the horse and leads him to the shoeing stand, a concrete slab under an awning in the far corner of the saddling pen. He ties the horse, pulls the shoeing box to him, bends over with a heavy sigh and picks up the foot.

"Freckles is lame."

"How bad?"

"Dead lame. I picked out his hoof, but I couldn't see anything."

"What's he carrying?"

"A baby saddle."

"Is Smokey rented?"

"Let me look. Yeah, Smokey's already going."

"Damn. Wait—what about Alvin?"

"Hold on. Nope, Alvin's open."

"There you go."

Donny scuttles out the tack room door. His whiskers twitch, rodent-like. He looks at the horses on the rail, checks out what Sam is doing, then darts back into the tack room and rifles through some papers at the desk, looking very intense and preoccupied and important. He soon tires of this, scuttles back out with a clipboard and begins writing the afternoon's private lesson assignments on the board in his cramped, half-legible scrawl. This is not a job that needs doing right now, but it keeps him from having to lift a saddle and put it on a horse. On busy mornings like this, much of Donny's time is spent in evasive maneuvers, designed to make him appear harried and overworked, poses and pantomimes that use up far more energy than actually doing something would.

The morning gradually lightens. The clouds are low and ominous. You can't see the hills above the lake, and this is a bad sign.

By seven AM the horses are saddled. A couple of wranglers are in the alley scooping horse manure into a wheel barrow, and a small wad of guests is gathered at the gate.

"Hey! Hey, partner!"

I have just tied a horse at the side rail. Beyond the fence stands a guy in shorts and a thick hooded sweatshirt with just his nose sticking out. He waves at me.

"Hey," he says, "what's the weather going to do?"

I peer skyward, and ponder the clouds. This is where I'm supposed to be the wise, experienced cowboy, expert on the country for miles around and privy to all its meteorological mysteries.

"Might rain," I pronounce, sagely.

"Really?"

"Might."

"If it rains do you still take the ride?"

I shrug. "You guys want to go, we'll go. Hardly anybody ever melts."

"Oh." It's hard to tell if this news reassures or disappoints.

"Someone will be at the gate in about fifteen minutes to check you folks in," I say, and turn to leave.

"Wait," he calls. "Do the parents *have* to go with the little kids, or can the kids go by themselves?"

There is the unmistakable rattle and clatter of a Dodge diesel, and Jake's battered pickup creeps into the lot. There are no parking spots left, all the spaces being occupied by BMWs and mini-vans and SUVs with bicycle racks, but Jake has never concerned himself with proper parking—or, for that matter, careful driving, a fact borne out by the scrapes, dents and contusions along both sides of his truck. He rolls on through, like a tugboat, scattering guests, and drifts to a stop at the alley gate. He sees me and gives a loose salute.

"It's a long row and a dull hoe," he announces. "You got anything to report, boy?"

He's eighty years old and thin as a toothpick, with a neat white mustache and brilliant blue eyes. Under the curled brim of his hat he is, as usual, grinning.

"It's a breakfast ride, Jake."

"I hope these boogers brung their slickers. You think they did?"

"It never rains in California, Jake."

"That's right, I forgot."

Jake has worked on this ranch in one capacity or another for over fifty years. Among the first wranglers to hire on when the guest ranch opened in 1946, he later helped run the cattle operation with the legendary cowman Mike Chrissman, and stocked the ranch dozens of times as a commission cattle buyer. For a while he ran the dude string as head wrangler, a job that fit him like the custom boots he wears. Nobody enjoys visiting and teasing the guests more than Jake, and for many he is the walking, talking personification of the ranch, ready to shake your hand and laugh over a corny joke or the middling bad cowboy poetry he writes. He's pretty much retired now, but the front office keeps him on the payroll as a public relations figure. His job is to show up, drink coffee, and be here when the dudes come through so they can bask in his radiance. Guests will return home and tell all their friends that the American Cowboy is alive and well and living at the Alamitos Ranch.

We head for the tack room, where Mark and Ray and Lisa are taking a breather before the onslaught begins. Donny hovers near the desk. Jake grabs himself a cup of coffee and props one foot up on a folding chair. His boots this morning are the black full-quill ostrich with the 14-inch bright green tops, almost neon. He sips at the coffee, turns the Styrofoam cup around and plucks at the rim, takes another sip, repeats the process.

"I hope everybody knows they're fixing to get wet," he says. "I's listening to the radio a while ago, and they say it's gonna be a frog-strangler."

Ray says, "You mean you're not riding with us, Jake?"

"I'm riding old diesel smoke this morning. But I get up there and it's raining, I ain't even getting out of the truck."

Ray says, "Man, them are some boots."

Jake laughs and tugs up a pant leg. "Ain't these the goddamnedest things?"

The phone rings. Donny snatches it up. His greeting is a nasal monotone. "Mmmm yes g'morning barn may I help you." He listens. "Yes, ma'am," he says. "We're still going, yes ma'am. No, we don't supply rain coats, I'm sorry."

He hangs up and takes a rubber hat cover from the side pocket of his thermal vest and begins stretching it over his battered straw Resistol. These covers, known around the barn as hat condoms, are either too large for your hat, and stick up around it in a translucent plastic cloud, or they're too small and cause the brim to curl up like a bad taco. Donny has found himself a small one, and struggles to get it fitted.

At the gate, the swarm of hopeful riders has grown. There are umbrellas in evidence, which is troubling. Umbrellas and horses don't mix, as a general rule. An umbrella is much too sudden and, if popped open while the user is in the saddle, will make a horse think a large predatory bird has just descended, causing terror and mayhem. Horses run when they are frightened, and will continue to run as long as the umbrella stays up there. That's usually not very long.

Sam stomps in. "Might as well get 'em started, Donny."

Donny leaps up, grabbing clipboards, pens and pencils, and scurries out.

"If it would just go ahead and start raining," Sam says, addressing the room and any stray weather gods who might be listening, "we could cancel this and save everyone a lot of headaches."

This is rhetorical, of course. It will never happen, and we know it. It never rains *before* a ride. It waits until you're out there as far as you can go, way out by the permanent pasture or the Indian Camp, and then explodes over you.

The crew heads outside to take up positions, and in a minute the first wave arrives, children running ahead—*"Don't run, Trevor, there's horses!"*—followed by parents, and Grandma and Grandpa with digital cameras and sensible shoes. They enter through the open corral gate and file to the mounting block, the kids jumping around, playing grabass and squealing, the parents chattering and laughing. A couple of the dads peer up at the sky and look worried. Some have come prepared for the weather; there are raincoats and mufflers and ski gloves. One seventh grader has shown up in a ball cap and a Pink Floyd T-shirt, apparently believing that a curled lip and arrogant attitude are all he needs to protect him from the elements. Jake greets them all.

"By golly, about time you showed up!"

"Howdy, Jake! You think it'll rain?"

"You betcha!"

Now comes the terrifying process of getting these dudes mounted. Terrifying for us, I mean. Most of the guests are happily ignorant of the perils in having so many large ranch animals moving around the same area with amateurs on their backs.

Jake goes through the same thing every morning. The idea is that people will look at the white board, find their name written in Donny's spidery scribble, and directly to left of their name will be the name of the horse assigned to them. Jake points to a candidate.

"Who're you riding?"

"I don't know."

The white board is roughly the size of a freeway exit sign. For some folks it's hard to see. Jake jerks a thumb.

"Look up there on the board."

The guest, a frazzle haired woman in pink capri pants and red sneakers with sparkles, squints. Blinks.

"Oh! I'm riding Cherokee."

"Cherokee!" Jake shouts. He points to the next victim. "How about you? Who're you tormenting today?"

"Gold Dust."

Jake hollers, "Gold Dust!"

And so it begins. As names are called the wranglers fan out across the corral. The horses stand waiting, heads down. Some might even be asleep, so remember to say something before you touch them. If you startle a horse, he could set back, fart and lunge forward, causing the two horses across from him to set back, fart and lunge forward, a nasty chain reaction that can travel all the way down the rail resulting in commotion and noise, and looking very unprofessional. So, speak to him softly, perhaps pet him on the neck. Untie and step him away from the rail. Check the saddle—sometimes they can slip. Snug the cinch, take the halter rope and lead him to the mounting block, where you dispense directions.

"Okay, stick your left foot in this stirrup, grab that saddle horn and swing your leg over. No, no! Use the other foot."

"Really? But I'm right-handed."

"Use that foot you'll wind up sitting backwards."

"Oh."

"That's it. Good job. Now go ahead and pick up your reins. Those leather things right there. I'm going to lead him off a little ways and we'll adjust the stirrups for you."

"Ooooh! He's moving!"

"Yes, ma'am, they do that."

After adjusting the stirrups and giving the rudimentary steering lesson—left, right, *whoa!*—you send your dude across the alley to the sorting pens, where Sam separates all comers according to their professed abilities: beginner, intermediate or the terrifying advanced.

Go back and get another one.

The wind has picked up. It has grown a set of teeth.

Eventually all the riders are in the saddle, looking expectantly around, ready for the next thing to happen. Of the 60 who signed up, 34 have chosen to brave the coming storm. And it's coming, too, that's for damn sure. No one wearing a skin can have any doubt. The morning has turned solid gray. The lenses of every pair of eyeglasses in the corral are speckled with moisture. The air chuffs around, whipping through mane and horse tail. The kid in the Pink Floyd T-shirt is trying to keep his ball cap from blowing off by mashing it against his head with one hand. He's wearing it backwards, of course, which makes as much sense as anything else around here. Sam stands in the alley and, sounding very much like a drill instructor, addresses them.

"People, people! Listen up! It is going to rain, all right? It is going to *rain*. If you ride these horses up there, you gotta ride them back. *In the rain*. You can't go bailing off on us halfway. It gets dangerous if we have to lead a bunch of horses back."

He pauses. Blank stares from the participants.

"If you are not comfortable with this scenario, the time to get off is now."

Hands on hips, he waits for some kind of response. He gets nothing. They all believe he's talking to somebody else.

"Okay! You can't say I didn't warn you!" He shakes his head and, almost to himself, adds, "Just because you can afford to stay here doesn't make you smart."

The wranglers rush back to the tack room, in search of rain slickers. We all have one, someplace, and eventually we find them and put them on. Some are bright yellow, shiny and new, right out of the Cabela's catalog. Others are stained with mildew and look as if they've been wadded up in a forgotten corner since the last rain, which is probably the case. Ray has a stiff oilskin coat from Australia that drags the ground. He struggles to move around in it.

After pulling up our britches and taking a collective deep breath, we bridle our own horses and swing aboard. Sam sends the first set of five riders into the alley, like loading bullets into a gun, and Ray trots out to get in front of them. Lisa and Donny are on the ground, moving down the line getting a final pull on the cinches.

Sam shouts, "Okay! You're set!"

They head down the alley and vanish into the mist. Sam sorts out the next group of five. Tyrell nudges his horse to the head of the line.

"Okay! Good to go!"

I end up with a father and two little boys on an intermediate ride. The boys are seven and eight, somewhere in there, and according to Dad belong on an intermediate ride rather than a beginner ride because they're savvy little buckaroos who've ridden before, twice if you count the pony ring at the county fair, and besides that the beginner ride only walks along, which is boring. A woman in a parka brings up the rear, riding a white horse named Eagle, and I assume, at first, she's mother to this clan. Then I think maybe not. She rocks along, staring straight ahead, both hands gripping the horn, and pays no attention to the kids, or Dad, or anything else, including her horse.

Dad says, "Kyle, is your jacket zipped up? Kevin, look and see if your brother's coat is zipped."

"How many pancakes are you going to eat, Daddy?"

"I don't know."

"I'm going to eat a lot of pancakes. I'm going to eat sixteen pancakes. Or seventeen. With syrup!"

"You're not going to eat just pancakes. You'll eat something healthy along with them. Maybe some fruit."

"I want hot chocolate, too. Are you going to have hot chocolate?"

"I don't know."

"Daddy?"

"What?"

"I'm cold."

"Well, zip up your jacket."

We creep along the road, through the groaning automatic gate and past the turn-off to the Staircase Trail. It's already wet enough that I don't trust the footing over there, all slick clay along the creekbank. I stick to the shoulder beside the gravel road, and even pick up a trot for about a hundred yards and let the kids giggle and bounce.

The Sand-hill Trail has better drainage and is safer going, so we peel off there and snake our way up the slope through a cluster of oak trees, and onto the flat. To our right, the clouds have blotted out not only the hills, but the lake itself has disappeared, and you could throw a rock into it from here with little effort. It's a bit scary.

Beyond the flat we catch the road again where it loops around the hill, and now a quarter mile of ridge line spins out, the highest, most exposed and nastiest stretch on the whole route. I'm hoping to make it across before things fall totally apart, but of course it's here, the worst possible spot, that the storm decides to bite us.

The wind, tired of fiddle-farting around with all this gusting and swirling, turns angry. And serious. It tears at my hat. I pull the brim down around my ears and suck my head into my coat, like a turtle. The rain hits, whipped by the wind, stinging and cold, and instantly all the horses behind me whirl around with their butts to the storm. One of the kids yelps.

"Whoa!" Dad shouts, "whoa—whoa!"

He pulls high and hard on the reins, sucking his horse backwards across the road.

"Lower your hand!" I holler through the wind.

He can't hear me over his own shouts, and continues to yank on his horse's face. The horse continues backwards, leaving the road now and skidding towards a steep and slick cliffside that will drop him fifty feet straight down into the lake.

I scream, "*Lower your hand!*"

He lowers his hand. The horse stops, as if by magic.

"Wow," Dad says. "Oh, wow. That was scary." He looks at me. His hair is plastered against his forehead. Water drips from his nose. "When we get to the breakfast place, there's some kind of shelter, right?"

"Shelter?"

"Yeah. You know, just until this lets up a little."

I look at the sky. Or try to. The rain beats me in the face, causing me to lose enthusiasm. "I don't think it's going to let up."

"You don't?"

It must be understood that to weanie out because of bad weather is a shameful thing for a wrangler. It just isn't done. No matter how much you might stew and grumble under your breath, no matter how cold the water running down your neck, pride is involved, and be it earthquake or lightning or gale force winds, you've got to cowboy up, and wrangle tough. You can't even mention the possibility of turning back. The guests are free to suggest it, though, and wranglers are allowed to be happy when they do. You can then return in absolution, with no stain upon your soul. I wait for him to make the call.

He just sits there, getting wetter.

I prod a little. "Everybody okay?"

He blinks. "Yeah. Yeah, I guess."

The woman on Eagle has pulled up her hood. Other than this, she takes no notice of the weather, or the people around her. She stares off into the gray void.

Well, hell.

We press on.

We are headed for a spot romantically called the Adobe Camp, where for over eighty years stood an old adobe cabin, probably a caretaker's house or some sort of line shack–nobody knows anymore, and nobody actually ever camps there, in spite of what they call it. The original house was bulldozed several years ago and replaced with a shiny replica of itself, complete with a porch and ramada built of authentic barn wood shipped all the way from Texas. There are antique knick-knacks on the walls, a couple of mission style chairs, and taxidermy hung up here and there to scare the children. Outside is a covered kitchen area for cooking pancakes and serving bacon and tortillas, with three rows of picnic tables lined up in the gravel yard around it. In happier times people eat breakfast in sun-dappled shade, and kids frolic and squeal and play in the dry creek bed among the gray rocks and dusty sycamore leaves.

When we finally reach the picket line only fourteen horses are there ahead of us. They stand with lowered heads, rain streaked and miserable. Ray and Donny and Mark are hunkered under the same trees, hat brims wilting—even Donny's, whose hat condom appears to be leaking. They slog forward to help down my riders, who, as soon as their feet touch the muddy ground, flee wordlessly in the direction of the adobe.

"Lisa turned back," Donny informs me. He sounds miffed. "I seen her, she was at the top of the Bohannon trail and she just turned around and went home. Just turned around."

The adobe is a disaster area, more like the scene of a third world calamity than a happy dude ranch activity gone bad. Guests are huddled on the porch, inside the house itself peering out through the screen door, under the roofed kitchen area, borrowing towels from the staff, the little ones they use on the tables, to wipe their children down. Children are crying. Wives are chewing on husbands. Husbands are looking around for someone they can hold responsible for this outrage. The cooks and servers stand under the dripping eaves, wondering why they didn't go into the construction business with their cousin's husband when they had the chance. No one is interested in pancakes.

The barn truck fishtails to a stop in the mud outside the fence. Sam climbs out, and is immediately accosted by half a dozen guests who demand to know the meaning of this.

"Why is everyone so surprised? I warned you, didn't I?"

Donny sidles up to him. "Lisa turned back, Sam. She—"

"I know she did, Donny. She's one of the few in this whole mess showing any sense."

A white van from the lake pulls up beside Sam's truck. A great cry arises from the multitude. People surge forward, like refugees rushing the helicopters at the fall of Saigon.

"*No!*" Sam shouts. "No fair sneaking back in the van! If you rode a horse up here you have to ride him back!"

Nobody pays any attention to him. I hear a mother directing her little girl: "Just get in the van, don't tell anyone. Don't say anything, just go."

Another van pulls up behind the first. The front office has ignored Sam's wishes and decided to mount a rescue. Sam continues to curse and shout and flap his arms, but it's no use. The cause is lost. In the end, over half the horses are abandoned, and we all have to drag a string of them back to the barn. All of us except Ray.

"Ol' Gus won't lead nobody," he grins, nodding toward his horse, a crotchety antisocial sorrel gelding with pig-small eyes. "Sorry!"

He leads home most of the brave soggy riders who have elected to stick it out. I wind up with four riderless horses, lead ropes bowlined to the horse in front, bowlined to the horse ahead of that one, all with their ears pinned back and wanting to crab and fight with each other the whole way. The only rider I have with me is the woman on Eagle.

The wind and rain continue to pound.

Halfway back, from under her hood, the woman says, "I don't mind riding in the rain. If it's not too cold."

Out of nowhere she makes this statement. I didn't even know she could talk. I don't respond, because I can't think of a response, except to tilt my head forward and allow the water to pour off my hat.

"It's kind of romantic," she says. And then, "Could we gallop a little?"

DEPUTY MCGREW

W E GOT OURSELVES a new Sheriff's deputy out here, and it turns out Rodney Duncan is afraid of cops. I never knew that—hardly anybody did. It's a real phobia with him, like when people are scared to death of heights or spiders, or clowns. It makes you wonder how a thing like that gets started. Maybe his mother was frightened by a policeman when she was carrying him. Hard to say.

Of course, Rodney wasn't the first to meet this new deputy. I was, the morning she knocked me down and handcuffed me. It was quite a shock.

I was headed for Academy Feed to get a load of hay cubes. What happened was, I stopped at Larry's Market on the way, for some gas and a cup of coffee, and Larry has that coffee maker of his turned up too hot. Good coffee, but you could clean an engine block with that stuff. It's like molten lava. Larry is a Sikh fella. That's a religion they got over there in the Mideast, and you have to wear a turban if you belong to it. He wears one every day. He and his wife Anita run this little store and gas station, and just work their tails off. I like them a lot, but Larry needs to throttle that coffee machine down a touch.

The new deputy must have been parked behind the *Booth Ranches* sign on Hills Valley Road, the one next to the big propane tanks. I didn't see her. About the time I passed the sign, the plastic lid popped off that coffee cup and half of it went into my lap, and my driving became reckless. I let go of the wheel and threw the Styrofoam cup on the floor, tried to stand upright at the same time, only to look up and realize that I was headed straight for the bar ditch. I grabbed the wheel again and swerved back across the road. She flicked on her red light and swung in behind me, but I wasn't paying attention to anything but my burned parts. She hit me with the siren, and even then it was a few seconds before I noticed. I was already pulling off to the shoulder. I jumped from the truck and jigged around and cussed and swatted at my drenched jeans.

She hollered, "Please get back in your vehicle, sir!"

"Ouch ouch oh hell and damn oh God bless America," I explained.

"Sir! Please return to your vehicle! Now!"

"Ouch ouch ouch," I said, continuing my dance, scalded clean to the pin feathers. "Holy cow, holy *cow!*"

"I won't ask again, sir!"

"I ain't getting back in there, it's wet and it's on fire—"

"Sir!"

"Go to hell!"

She must have thought I was out of my mind, and I guess I was, sort of. I don't know how she got to me so quick or what kind of king fu maneuver she used, but all at once the ground came up and hit me in the face. I got a mouthful of dirt, and her knees were in the small of my back and both my hands were sucked behind me and I felt those metal bracelets snick around my wrists. Like I say, it was a shock.

"Let me see some identification," she said.

"What are you doing?"

"Stop struggling, sir! I need you to stop struggling!"

"You're standing on my spine!"

"Quiet *down!*"

"I don't know what this is about—I spilled my coffee. . ."

"I warned you, sir! I will taze you!"

That was enough for me. I didn't want her zapping me with any taser. I've seen that on television, and when they hit you with one of those things it makes you flop down and quiver like a landed trout. I went limp. She leaned over and shouted into my ear, "Are you going to give me trouble? If I let you up are you going to stay calm and not fight me?"

"I don't know what this is about."

"Sir! Do you understand what I'm saying to you?"

Through clenched teeth I promised to act nice. At that point I would have agreed to mow her lawn for a year, or clean out her garage, anything to get her off me. It was plain I wasn't posing much of a problem for her. She was just an average sized woman, not muscled up or anything, but she put a hand under my arm and jerked me to my feet as if I weighed no more than a hamster.

She asked again for ID, and I told her it was in my left hip pocket and she was welcome to it, but she'd have to get it herself. She fished my wallet out, removed my license and inspected it, glaring with suspicion at me and then at my picture and back again. Maybe I was a criminal kingpin in a thirty-year-old truck, and a master of disguise to boot. She left me there, handcuffed by the side of the road in front of God and everyone while she went to her car and radioed in to check me for outstanding warrants or whatever it is they do. After a few minutes she came back. I thought she looked a little miffed that I wasn't wanted for anything.

"Do you know why I stopped you?"

"You didn't stop me. I spilled hot coffee on myself and pulled over to get out and scream."

She was in her mid-thirties, with dark hair drawn tight behind her head, and a prominent jaw. Her eyes were blue, and piercing. Not hard-looking, but she had an edge to her. Of course, that might just be my take on it, since she'd so recently whipped my ass. The little tag she wore over her badge said her name was Deputy McGrew.

She went to my truck and looked inside at the wet seat, and the white coffee cup on the floor, and probably caught the smell of burnt flesh, all good evidence I was telling the truth. She came back and removed the cuffs and handed me my wallet and license.

"You haven't been drinking this morning, have you, sir?"

"Just that damned coffee."

"Are you under the influence of any narcotic, any mind-altering drug or anything like that?"

"The only mind-altering thing I've experienced is getting thrown to the ground and jumped on."

"The way you were screaming and wriggling around is consistent with someone hopped up on a controlled substance. An officer can't be too careful. Hold still and watch my finger here. Track it with your eyes. I need to look at your pupils."

"My pupils are fine."

"Watch my finger, please."

I thought she was going to put me through an entire field sobriety test, but in the end she just wrote me a ticket for distracted driving, and by the time she handed me the pen and pointed at where I was supposed to sign, my britches had cooled down but I was plenty hot under the collar. I kept my head, though, and never mouthed off. No point giving her an excuse to hurl me back onto the gravel.

It was all over the valley, of course, by the time I got home from the feed store. My wife had already received half a dozen calls from people wanting to know why I'd been arrested and was I going to prison and what in the world had I been up to. It's amazing how quick these things get blown out of shape.

That was the beginning.

Three days later Doris Sousa ran into my truck with her husband's brand-spanking new Chevrolet three-quarter ton.

There'd barely been enough time for my seat covers to dry out. I was downtown at the post office mailing some packages when I heard the crunch. A traffic collision, even at low speed, has an unmistakable sound, and like everyone else up and down the block I hurried outside to see what happened. Lo and behold, here was Dale Sousa's shiny new silver crew-cab hung up on the rear bumper of my old Ford. Doris climbed down from behind the wheel and came to me waving her hands in distress, as if trying to shake the bad luck off her fingers.

"Oh, damn, damn, damn!" she said. "I can't see over the hood of this thing. I couldn't tell where your truck ended and the parking spot began." She laughed a little, that tight, nervous sort of laughter you sometimes hear in church or at funerals.

Doris is in her late fifties, barely five-foot-tall even in her cowboy boots. She has wild, curly hair, and is built very much like a pear. She was trembling, and white as a ghost.

I said, "Are you okay, Doris? Did you hurt yourself?"

"No, no, I'm okay. Just, you know, my heart fluttering. I don't think I was even going five miles an hour. Oh, God, how bad is it?"

I knelt and inspected the damage. Somehow, she'd missed hitting me with the Chevy's heavily armored bumper, and crumpled her front quarter-panel on the passenger side. Not real bad. It wasn't shoved clean to the tire, like sometimes happens. But bad enough.

"Can I still drive it?"

"I think so. You better call Dale and see where he wants to take it."

She gasped, and put a hand against her lips. "Oh, no. I can't do that. Oh, God, no."

"He's got his phone with him, doesn't he?"

"I can't. I can't call him. I just can't. He'll go crazy. Him and Fred left this morning for Arizona. They're looking at some stock trailers a man has for sale there. If I call him, he'll just lose his mind. We've only had this truck barely a month, and I wasn't supposed to be driving it. Can you help me get it to Rodney's?"

"Rodney's? Rodney doesn't do body work."

"But he'll know where to take it, won't he? He'll know what to do. Please?"

When a lady is shook up that badly and asks you please in such a trembly little voice, you really don't have a say in it anymore. I told her all right, I'd follow her over there and give her a ride home after, if she needed it. She could have asked me to beat a chicken with a baseball bat and I'd have probably done that too. I'm kind of a pushover.

"I didn't hurt your truck too bad, did I?"

"Looks like you broke my tail light, is all."

"Oh! I'm so sorry."

"It's no big whoop. I can fix that easy."

I followed her out of town and we hooked a left onto Hills Valley Road. I thought Doris was making a mistake, but what can you do? It was her mistake to make. I knew Dale was a crusty old dairy farmer and could be loud and pushy sometimes, especially after he got a few beers in him, but it wasn't like he'd ever raise a hand to her. He'd just yell is all, but heck, anybody would, a new truck like that. Then it would be over and he'd get it fixed and that would be the end of it.

I glanced in my rearview, and was surprised to see Deputy McGrew's cruiser right on my hind end. She just appeared out of nowhere, poof, like a magical trick, and her red light was on. Again. I pulled over, thinking what the hell, but smart enough to stay put inside the truck this time. I remembered she was touchy about that. I cranked down my window and pretty quick here she came, her visored hat tugged squarely down on her head and her ticket book out and at the ready.

"Deputy McGrew," I said. "We got to stop meeting like this."

"Excuse me?"

"Never mind. I was just—never mind."

"You turned that corner back there I noticed you have a brake light not working. Were you aware of that?"

I said yes, and told her it had only happened five minutes ago. I described the little fender-bender and said I planned on getting it fixed right away, and so forth, babbling on and on like an idiot. She stared at me.

"You were involved in an accident and didn't bother to report it?"

"Well," I said. I cleared my throat. It felt dry all of a sudden. "You couldn't call it an accident, hardly. Not really. It's just a little old tail light."

"May I see your license, please?"

"Don't you remember what it looks like from the last time?"

"Take it out of the wallet, please."

I gave it to her, and dragged out my registration and insurance card and handed them over as well, and she took them back to the cruiser and got on the radio again, I guess to find out if I'd committed any major crimes in the last three days.

You would think, after slamming me to the ground and kneeling on me last time, she might cut me a little slack on the broken tail light deal. Wouldn't you think that? I sure did. But no. Hell no. She returned in a few minutes with a fix-it ticket all made out, and had me sign it with her sputtery little Bic ballpoint and presented me with a copy, then proceeded to lecture me how it was my civic duty to report any and all traffic collisions and accidents, and I should keep this in mind for the future.

I was still riled up when I got to Rodney's barn. Doris and Rodney were outside in the gravel lot waiting for me, Rodney with his big belly and blue coveralls and his cowboy hat. The drooping walrus mustache he sported had gotten grayer since I'd seen him last, or maybe he'd just run out of his Grecian Formula for Men.

Rodney was a mechanic, and a darn good one. His barn was painted bright red, a solid hip-roofed building across the yard from his house, and there was a pen full of goats out behind that, and a couple of Holstein drop calves stumbling around in a scrabbly pasture, and the requisite half-dozen chickens pecking away at the dirt. This was the place all the locals brought their sick trucks and cars. For a while Rodney ran a garage in town, but the gang-banger kids kept breaking in at night and stealing his tools, so he closed that place and started working at home instead. He had a hydraulic lift in there, and a chain fall for pulling engines, and an air compressor and a swamp cooler, and he didn't charge you an arm and a leg like they do everywhere else. He looked a little worried right now.

He said, "I told her I don't do body work."

"I told her that, too."

Doris said, "Where did you go? I thought you were right behind me."

I explained about Deputy McGrew and how I now had a second ticket to match the first one she'd given me.

"I'm glad it was you and not me," Rodney said, and a kind of haunted look came into his eyes. "That wouldn't be good. Not good at all." Then he grinned. "I ain't fond of police. They scare the hell out of me."

"Really? How come?"

He shrugged. "Who knows? They just do. I see one and my heart goes to pounding and I get all sweaty, even when they ain't looking at me."

"That's weird."

"It sure is. But I can't help it."

Doris said, "Could you at least look at this truck, Rodney? Maybe there's something you could do."

Rodney took his hat off and scratched his bald head, and went over and looked at the crumpled quarter-panel. He stroked his mustache and lighted a cigarette and smoked it for a while, and looked at the damage some more, all thoughtful and sad.

"It ain't like it used to be, you know," he said, addressing his remarks to me. "You don't tap the dents out with your mallet and smear Bondo over everything no more. It's remove and replace these days, everything's pressed out of fiberglass and plastic, all pre-made. Your old-time body and fender man is a relic of the past."

"Isn't there someone you can call who might help?" Doris pleaded.

"Yeah," I said, "you know a bunch of old relics, don't you, Rodney?"

He flicked his cigarette butt at me, but missed. "Pop that hood for me, will you?"

I climbed into the Chevy and fumbled around until I located the lever, cunningly hidden, that released the hood latch. He raised the hood and found a step-stool and climbed up and had a look, but all I could see was wires and shrouds and so forth. You couldn't spot an engine in there at all, though I suppose it had one.

Rodney said, "You'd be better off taking it to the dealership, Doris."

"Oh, I can't. Dale would find out, they'd call him up first thing to ask some sort of question, and then he'd know."

"He's going to know sooner or later, ain't he?"

"Oh, lordy, I hope not. I was hoping you could hurry up and fix it before he got home and he'd never be the wiser."

Rodney raised his bushy eyebrows. "You'd still have to order the quarter-panel from the dealer, and even if they had it in stock, I don't have a paint booth here."

"Isn't there somebody around who does? Don't you have a friend who could paint it real quick?"

"Well, Doris, I don't know. I don't know." He looked at me. "Didn't Mark Hendrixson rig up a deal in his equipment shed last winter so he could paint his own tractor? I know he's got some paint guns over there."

I shook my head. "I don't know why you're asking me. This is all starting to sound a little crazy."

"How long is Dale out of town for?"

It wound up with Rodney telling Doris to leave the truck with him and he'd make some calls and see what he could do. No promises, he said, but as far as Doris was concerned the end of the world had just been postponed, and she could breathe again. She clapped her hands together and bounced up and down like a little kid, and I think she would have kissed him except she couldn't reach that high.

I drove her home. On the way I tried one more time to tell her it was a screwy way of doing things, but I might as well have been speaking to my wife's cats, all the good it did. She just talked over the top of me, rattling on about some nephew of hers who'd lost his job and had to go to Alaska, though she wasn't clear on exactly why, her voice all fast and high-pitched and nervous, so you could tell she was still pretty worried and trying to pretend she wasn't. I dropped her off at the dairy, figuring I'd done my neighborly duty and that was that. I wished her luck. It's hard to talk sense to somebody who isn't listening.

Two days later she called me up in a panic. She didn't say hello or good morning or who was calling, she just wailed, "What am I going to do?"

"Doris?"

"He came back early!"

"Dale did?"

"Yes, Dale. He couldn't make a deal with the man in Arizona who had those trailers, and they couldn't find any others they liked, so he and Fred jumped in the car and drove all night to get home, all the way from Flagstaff. They got in about six o'clock this morning, and the first thing he did was see his truck wasn't there. He called the Sheriff's Department and reported it stolen. Stolen! What am I going to do?"

"You're going to have to tell him, Doris."

"I know, I know. I can't tell him nothing right now. He's not here. Him and Fred are out driving around, looking for it. He didn't even wait and drink a cup of coffee first, or eat a piece of toast or nothing."

"Did you call Rodney?"

"Oh, I tried, but that man, he never answers his phone. He just lets it go to voicemail every time. How can somebody be in business and not take phone calls?"

I hung up and drove to Rodney's. He was just backing Dale's truck out onto the gravel lot, and if I hadn't known it got wrecked, I'd never have believed it. The crunched quarter-panel was replaced and the paint was shiny and new. He had rigged up a makeshift paint booth in the barn, and covered the walls in Visqueen and hosed everything down to keep the dust out of the air.

"I told you Hendrixson had them paint guns," he said. "He lent them to me and never charged me a dime. Pretty good, huh? It took a day for them boys at Walden's Chevrolet-GMC to get the paint in stock, but after that it was a piece of cake."

"I didn't think the dealer would sell that brand-new stuff to an independent garage."

"You just got to know who to talk to. I'm friends with Kiki there at the parts desk. He takes good care of me."

He said it wasn't hard to change out the quarter-panel, just some screws and clips and brackets and a few swear words. Probably didn't take three hours, he said. "I been wanting to work on one of these babies since they came out. Jump in the passenger seat. I need to take her for a test drive and make sure nothing's rattling."

I knocked the dust from my boots and climbed in. Of course I did. I'd never ridden in a truck that new. It was like sitting down at some gentleman's club in London or New York City, with creamy leather seats, and dark imitation wood grain everywhere, the only thing missing was the butler shuffling around with the drink tray. It smelled good in there, so I guess Dale hadn't smoked any of his cigars in it yet. There was a big computer console in the middle you could work just by touching it with your finger.

"It's got more computer to it than it does engine," Rodney said, as we pulled onto American Avenue and headed west between the orange groves. He barely touched the accelerator and it hurled me deep into my seat. Computer or not, it had plenty of power.

Rodney said, "Roll that window and see can you hear any noise. I bet you can't."

He was just as proud as if he'd invented the whole idea of a pickup in the first place. He handed me his nasty old Stetson and stuck his head out the window to listen as we rumbled along. "Tight as a drum," he said.

We drove all the way to the Minkler Cash Store, swung around in the parking lot and headed back.

I said, "You know Dale got home last night. Or this morning, rather."

"Really? I thought we had another couple days. I suppose Doris finally had to tell him what happened to his truck, didn't she?"

"No. I don't believe she did."

"You're kidding."

"Matter of fact, he called the sheriff and told them somebody stole it."

We drove along. Rodney rolled the window up and put his hat back on. "You might have mentioned this before."

"Sorry."

"She never told him? How could she not tell him?"

We made a right turn onto Cove Road. It ran for three miles or so, straight as a string along the foothills and flat as an ironing board, except for that humpy wooden bridge where it crossed the canal. There were tidy little places along here, row after row of olive trees, and lemon groves, and Rossi's pasture with his scrubby looking roping steers pressed up against the bob-wire fence.

Rodney said, "I need to put this truck in the barn and call Dale to come get it. This whole deal's getting ridiculous."

All of a sudden, things felt different. The cushy interior was no longer as warm and comfortable as it had been only five seconds ago. The sense of luxury and decadence had faded, replaced with a humming sort of tension.

Then Rodney said, "Oh, hell."

"What?"

He was peering hard into the mirror. "Cop back there, I think."

I swiveled around. "Where?"

"Right there behind us, where do you think he is? Ain't that a light bar on the roof?"

There was a vehicle back there, all right, way back there, too far off to make out any details except that it was white. And they *were* painting cop cars white these days, which I considered a dirty trick and totally unfair. When they were all black and white you could spot them easier, and a fella had a fighting chance to slow down and start obeying traffic laws and acting innocent before they pulled you over.

"Maybe he ain't seen us yet," Rodney said. "I'm going to hang a right up here and go out through Doug Brown's orange trees."

"Why don't we just head for your place? It's only a couple miles."

"Doggone it anyway."

He punched it, and that big old diesel picked up and ran, gaining twenty mile an hour in two seconds, so smooth and quick it took my breath. I thought we might be airborne any second. Sure enough, behind us the red light came on. Way the hell back there, but you couldn't miss it.

"Yep," I said, "it's a cop."

"Oh, Jeez. Oh, no."

"We probably ought to pull over, don't you think?"

We swerved right onto American Avenue, whipping past the stop sign with the spray paint on it like it wasn't even there, and zigged across the pavement and skidded left onto the dirt road between Brown's orange grove and the irrigation district's reservoir, bouncing and jouncing in our fine leather seats. Rodney was hunkered over the wheel, sweating, eyes wide open behind his smeared glasses.

We bucked and jerked through mudholes and over ruts and gullies, swerved around a stack of empty orange crates, then turned down between a row of trees, but it was too narrow for this behemoth of a truck, the branches scraping and slapping against the sides, whipping at the mirrors, etching Rodney's new paint into abstract art.

"This can't be good," I said, "this ain't good at all."

Rodney wasn't listening anymore. He wasn't talking, he was just gone. And he never slowed down. I could hear the siren now—and, somewhere off in the opposite distance, an answering siren, headed toward us. Like they were calling to each other. We were going to wind up on the six o'clock news. A gaggle of laborers were working among the trees up ahead with loppers and saws, and we burned right through the middle of them. Never hit anybody, thank goodness, but we sure scattered them. They hollered at us, and flipped us off and shook their fists, and I couldn't blame them a bit.

We squirted out onto some nameless little back road near the edge of town, but with that dust cloud roiling into the sky behind us we might as well have sent up a flare. John Dillinger we weren't. I craned around, watching, knowing what was coming, and saw the cruiser make the corner off American Avenue, lights ablaze and siren screaming like a peppered coyote.

I said, "Anywhere around here is fine if you want to let me out."

Rodney hunkered tighter around the wheel and gave that truck another goose. The tires broke traction and the rear end fishtailed around. We went maybe three hundred yards, and then a tractor and spray rig lumbered out from the trees and Rodney had to stomp the brake and crank the wheel hard to the right. We skidded off the road and into one of Brown's orange trees, and the airbags whumped open and knocked us both silly.

We climbed out just as the sheriff's cruiser slid to a halt thirty yards away. I heard chirping and tweeting all around me, but I didn't see any birds. I was dizzy, too. Deputy McGrew opened her door and crouched behind it and pointed her pistol at us.

"On the ground! Face down with your hands on your head. Now!"

Her back-up arrived half a minute later. They cuffed the two of us and stuck us in Deputy McGrew's car, and she drove us up to the hoosegow in Fresno.

"Somehow I knew it was going to be you," Deputy McGrew told me.

"I was thinking the same thing," I said.

I told her she needed to call Doris Sousa. I bet I said it six different times. Doris would clear this up in two shakes, just pick up the phone and give her a ring. "She hired Rodney to fix that truck, see, he never stole nothing. She run into me and broke my tail light—remember, you give me the fix-it ticket. Remember?"

I kept waiting for Rodney to chime in and back me up, but he was no help. He sat there staring straight ahead, as frozen stiff as a guy could get.

Deputy McGrew, sounding smug, said, "And I suppose once we have the proper warrants in hand and roll to your home locations we won't find all the evidence we need."

"Evidence of what?"

"We've had a rash of vehicle thefts in this particular area. At least two a week, regular as clockwork. I'm thinking we're close to clearing it up. Very close. Anything you want to say about that?"

"Not while I'm handcuffed in a cop car. Try me again later."

Let me tell you, it's uncomfortable to sit in one of those cruisers with your hands cuffed behind you. You have to lean way forward and it's hard on your back, and after a while your arms go to sleep on you. Deputy McGrew ushered us into the Sheriff's station and sat us on a hard bench, also uncomfortable, and went away and left us there for quite some time. When you're training a horse this technique is called soaking, and they let us soak there for better than an hour. Eventually Deputy McGrew came back and said she'd called Doris Sousa.

"Well, good!" I said. "She told you how it was, right?"

"She said she was shocked and disappointed."

"Hold on. Wait a minute. What did she say?"

"She said she was crushed that two people she knew, and considered friends, could do such a thing."

"Doris said that? Doris Sousa? You sure it was the right Doris Sousa you called?"

After that they took our names down and started writing their reports and filling out their forms. They have a machine for taking your fingerprints these days, an electronic gizmo they use instead of the old ink pads. That was interesting. I figured, well, this was it, my life was over and I was going into the system, and become a convicted felon who'd never get to own guns anymore or vote in elections, and my grandkid would be so ashamed and traumatized over it she'd quit school and drift off into drug addiction and homelessness and never speak to me again and my wife would divorce me and marry somebody else, probably that twerp Nathan Hollister she dated in high school before I knew her, and all this because Doris didn't want to tell her husband she wrecked his truck.

Just as they were fixing to stick us in a holding pen, Dale Sousa called them and straightened out the whole mess. He'd come home to find Doris at the kitchen table, crying, and he managed to holler the truth out of her. They had to let us go. Deputy McGrew acted real resentful about it. A few days later Doris phoned, and invited me and Rodney over to the house for supper, so she could try and make it up to us. I don't know if Rodney's going or not. I haven't called her back yet. I might. Maybe. I ain't decided yet.

THE CHICKEN STORY

T HIS ISN'T REALLY about the peacock, but that's when it all started. With the peacock.

You see, nature does not care. That's the main thing. It absolutely does not give a single hair on a rat's patootie. Some people think they can bend nature to their will, but this works out less than seldom. Others believe, if they treat nature with kindness, it will smile on them in gratitude, and wag its tail like an obedient dog, lay down at their feet and be nice to them in return. This doesn't work either. Nature just trundles along and does what it's going to do. It doesn't care.

This was a lesson we already knew. But we had to re-learn it, after the peacock showed up.

I was working in the mountains at the time. One evening I called home. Melissa said, "We have a new friend."

"What new friend?"

"A peacock. He's visiting the horses."

"A what?"

"He flew up on the back fence and spread his tail out, and the horses had a fit. You should have seen the dust flying!"

"They didn't tear down the fence, did they? Tell me they didn't tear down the fence."

"No, but they got really, really excited. They'd never seen anything like that."

"Why," I asked, "is there a peacock?"

She said the peacock was Aunt Peggy's.

Well. Of course it was.

Peggy was not precisely an aunt, but that's what everybody called her. She was a relation of some sort—Melissa's mother's second cousin's niece or something, whatever that made her to us. Some kind of relative, but distant enough that you still liked her. She had a habit of collecting strange animals and strewing them around her yard—even a llama, for a while, until it spit at her and she got rid of it. She lived down the hill from our place, next to the creek, and apparently the peacock was camped out on her roof. There'd been a couple of pea-hens, too, originally, but the coyotes had mucked them out in short order.

"That's why he's coming up here," Melissa said. "He's lonely."

At the end of September, we closed the pack station and I came home, and by then the horses and the peacock had made nice with each other. He spent his days strutting around the pasture with his tail fanned out, shaking and rattling it the way they do, and the horses had become bored with him. They paid him no more mind than they would a deer fly. Melissa bought a bag of scratch, and scattered a double handful on the ground for him a couple times a day, because everyone knows that when you're lonely you always feel better if you eat something. At night he flew back onto Aunt Peggy's roof to roost, and I was fine with that because it meant she had to clean up the mess and not me.

It went like this for a while, and then the fighting rooster arrived.

That's right, a real honest to goodness fighting chicken. At this point, why not?

Here is where mistakes were made.

Down the hill and across the road from Peggy's was a cluttered-up place under some eucalyptus trees, with two little houses on it. One of the houses had been rented to a Filipino gentleman who decided, one night, to leave suddenly. He kept a slew of fighting cocks in a bunch of little coops, and when he cleared them out, one of them got away, and I guess the guy couldn't spare the time to go after him.

This abandoned rooster fussed and scratched on his own for a few days, under the trees and along the creek. Melissa thought that, like the peacock, he got lonesome. I figured he just got hungry. He looked around, spotted the peacock hanging out with the horses at our place and thought, hey—if those people will feed a chicken that big, they'll feed anything. He bopped across the road and took up residence. He didn't bother to ask, or sit for an interview or fill out a rental agreement or anything. He merely arrived, and pecked at the earwigs in the wood pile, and fluffed and preened himself beside the peacock, and came running when Melissa scattered the cracked corn, and decided, all by himself, that I needed to be startled out of bed every morning at five AM with his raucous crowing. I don't understand how such a gigantic sound could erupt from such a small bird. It sounded like someone was strangling a goat outside our bedroom window, only louder.

Melissa thought he was cute, with his multi-colored feathers and lopsided comb and startled expression. He liked her, too, and would hang out while she worked in the yard, and come when she called him, and take naps on the porch while waiting for her to step outside and feed him some more.

He did not care for me. I think he saw me as a rival for affection and scratch grains, and began to scheme on how he might get rid of me. One morning he whanged into my legs and began beating me with his wings, and tried to sink his spurs into my shins.

"Hey!" I said, and booted him into the hay barn, where he rolled over three times and flapped away, squawking. I went into the house and got my pistol.

Melissa said, "Where are you going with that?"

"I am fixing to ventilate that rooster."

"No! Why would you shoot that poor defenseless chicken?"

I told her he had attacked me, and I wasn't going to stand for it. I pointed out with indignation the feather fluff and beak marks on my pant legs.

"What did you do? You must have done something to make him mad."

In the end, of course, she convinced me to put the pistol away and give the little bastard another chance. For the next few days he and I glared across the yard at each other with bitter suspicion, like two gunfighters in a saloon, but he gave me a wide berth.

Our two Doberman dogs were eyeing the rooster, too, but not with suspicion. They simply wanted to kill him—that old instinct to chase and chomp any stray critter that wandered into their territory. They'd never been around chickens, had never been taught to be tolerant of them.

"No, no!" Melissa cautioned, wagging a finger at them. "You be nice! You leave that rooster alone. No! No!"

The dogs would retreat, shooting resentful glances toward the chicken, disappointed they couldn't kill him this instant, with Mom standing there, and would have to wait for a more convenient time when no one was watching. The rooster just went on scratching and pecking, clueless as to how close to death he was at any given minute.

Ron the Horseshoer called me a week or so later. "Hey. You want some hens?"

I sighed. "Well, hell," I said. "Yeah, probably."

Ron the Horseshoer was one of my best friends. His wife and Melissa were riding buddies, and we spent a lot of Sundays at their place involved in fix-it projects and barbecues and beer drinking. He kept a dozen or so chickens himself, for the eggs, and every two or three years he'd get in a fresh bunch of pullets, and muck out the old hens. Usually he'd just wring their necks and throw them over the fence, but Melissa had told his wife about our rooster, and how he was lonely, and you can imagine where it went from there. Wouldn't it be nice for him, and so on.

We had a little equipment shed next to the hay barn, where I kept my oil cans and tow chains and cobwebs. I strung some poultry netting across the front, toted in a few milk crates filled with straw to serve as brooders, and Ron brought over a big dog crate full of hens. There were three Buff Orpingtons and three Barred Rocks, all stout and mature like old school teachers. They looked around, fluffed up their feathers, and settled in.

Within three days I was collecting eggs.

We'd raised some chickens when I was a kid. But I'd forgotten. For twenty years I had been forced to eat store-bought eggs, and didn't realize how dismal and pathetic my life had become. But these eggs—my God! They were smooth and buttery, with yokes so rich they were almost orange. Breakfast became a delight, something to look forward to, a reason to roll out of bed. I enjoyed gathering those eggs, too, mincing around the shed peering into the brooders and in the corners behind the oil cans, my own private Easter egg hunt. It was as if these darling hens were leaving me little presents every morning. In gratitude I bought cedar shavings to make them more comfortable, and a forty-pound sack of laying mash, and a brand-new plastic water dispenser from the Farm Supply store. I talked to them, and made silly cooing sounds when I fed them, and thought about giving them names. I became ridiculous. I didn't care. These were my girls.

I kept them locked in for a week or so, until they got used to their new digs, and then in the mornings let them out to fuss and scratch among the roses and berry vines. The rooster swooped in, and looked over his new flock like a sheik looking over his harem, and was delighted, too. The hens were all larger than him, but he didn't care. He preferred big girls.

He commenced to herd them about from here to there, puffing up his scrawny chest and flapping his wings and acting like a Mr. Biggity Pants. His world had taken a turn for the better. Everybody was happy. Even the peacock seemed content.

Melissa said, "You need to watch those dogs."

"What?" I said.

"They keep eyeing your chickens."

This time it was my turn to address the Dobermans. They were in the yard, watching the chickens. Salivating. I shook my finger at them, just as Melissa had, only this time it was Dad doing it. "No!" I said. "No! You leave those chickens alone. Do you hear me? No!"

The dogs slinked off. I went back inside, pleased with myself.

"Well?" Melissa said.

"I took care of it."

The rooster became more aggressive. His beady little eyeballs took on a feral, venomous look. He'd cast Melissa aside, the heartless cad, and now decided I was a rival and a threat for the affection of the hens, and I by-God must be put, once again, in my place. He began attacking me two or three times a day, hoping to drive me off. I never saw it coming, either. I would be minding my own business, working on the truck, or scooping horse poop, or just standing there, thinking about omelets, and suddenly he was on me, swatting and pecking, and I'd have to kick him across the yard again. He would tumble backwards, pick himself up and march away, satisfied that he'd made his point. It got tiresome after a while, but I had been warned against bringing out the firearms. I thought he was being seriously ungrateful, but it's hard to shame a chicken.

One evening about dusk Melissa came and found me. "That rooster is being mean to the Barred Rocks."

"Being mean? How?"

"He won't let them out of the corner. He's got them all bunched up there, and they're scared to move."

"Bunched where?"

She answered with those magic words all husbands know: "Go do something."

I went to the equipment shed—which I now thought of as The Coop–and had a look. The rooster was on one of the milk crate brooders, and had the Buff Orpingtons up there with him looking all chosen, and special. In the dark corner next to the rusty tow chains, the gray speckled Barred Rocks trembled in distress. They looked dejected and confused, if such things can be said about hens. When one of them tried to move toward the feeder, or get a drink from the brand-new plastic dispenser, the bastard rooster jumped down and pecked her back into submission.

Melissa was behind me. "See?"

"He doesn't like the Barred Rocks all of a sudden."

"He's a racist. He's a racist rooster."

I knocked him off the milk crate and re-established order. I made him stand in the corner, and see how he liked it, the little turd. The Barred Rocks went over and had a drink, and rejoined the Buffs. I wagged my finger and made threatening sounds, letting him know I wasn't about to stand for it. But when I returned after full dark with my flashlight, there he was, up on the milk crate with his golden-brown girls around him and the gray hens crammed in the corner again.

"What are you going to do about this?" Melissa demanded.

Well, to be honest, I didn't know what to do about it. I resorted to that old standard used by all husbands down through the centuries: "Don't worry. It'll be fine."

The point I'm hoping to make is what ended up happening was as much the rooster's fault as it was mine. I mean, I tried to be nice, and fair. I warned him. The fact that every time he came at me he got kicked into the sky should have told him something—even if your brain is the size of a pea, such experiences should leave an impression. Wouldn't you think?

I was near the horse pasture gate digging a hole with my trusty shovel when he attacked me for the last time. The shovel was the kind with the pointy end. I don't remember what the hole was for; I suppose Melissa needed something planted. If I looked a bit to my right, I could see the rose garden beside the house, and the six lovely hens fussing and scratching industriously between the bushes. The view warmed my heart. The peacock was in the pasture, shaking his tail at the horses, but I'd lost track of the rooster, and in fact hadn't given him a thought until I felt his scrawny body slam into my legs—so hard he almost knocked me down. For a little shit that hardly weighed four pounds, he sure meant it.

I kicked him away, as usual, but here he came right back, wings flapping. I felt his nasty beak stab me through my jeans, and I booted him again, rolling him into the fence. This seemed to enrage him even more, and he righted himself and charged one last time.

I swung the shovel.

I'll spare you the details. Let's just say when he came down this time it was all over. Mr. Rooster had gone to the happy chicken coop in the sky, and the hole I'd been digging was put to a different use than originally intended.

I felt bad about it. Sort of. But what could he expect? He had no business being so viciously disagreeable. I seem to remember the hens hopping up and down and clucking with relief when I told them, but I'm probably imagining that. I did think they'd be happier now, without him around to bully and peck and shove them into corners like some miniature dictator. I decided they were probably grateful to me, and rightly so. I had saved them from an abusive relationship. I was now cock of the walk, and they would reward me with even more eggs.

If you want to stop reading now, you can. It just goes seriously downhill from here.

Every evening, without fail, after the hens had filed inside and settled onto the cedar shavings for the night, we would proceed to the shed and count their beaks, then close the chicken wire door, satisfied that all were safe and accounted for. And, just as I figured, for the next week or so things were peaceful and quiet with the rooster gone. The hens flourished, and were happy. They got fatter, and more majestic, gliding about the place with a regal air, all of them, like feathered queens. I liked watching them, and watching over them. But you can't be everywhere at once.

One afternoon we had to go to town. Everybody has to go to town, sooner or later. Even people who like chickens. Supplies are needed, bills must be paid, errands run. We toddled off, and for whatever reason things ran late, and we weren't there to close the coop and count beaks. By the time we started for home it was after dark. We pulled into the drive, and as I got out to open the gate, the truck headlights illuminated a horrible scene.

There were feathered humps in the driveway. At least three of them. A couple more over there under the berry vines. Another against the fence. Motionless. They looked strangely pale in the truck lights. I didn't know what I was seeing at first, and then I realized. My heart sank.

My girls.

The dogs had got them.

The dogs had acted exactly like dogs, the same way the rooster had been a rooster and chickens were chickens. Nature. The dogs had seen their chance, and taken it. I looked for them, and found them cowering in the dog run. They only got locked in there when they'd been bad, like going to dog jail. They'd put themselves away on their own–they knew they'd done a terrible thing, but they couldn't help it. And it wasn't their fault. It was mine.

I gathered up my girls and, feeling hollow and guilty, buried them the next morning near the spot I'd planted the rooster. But not too close. As I tamped down the dirt, the peacock glided up to see what I was doing.

"Well, bucko," I said. "Looks like you're on your own again."

He blinked, and fanned out his tail in full iridescent display. He stood there, rattling those feathers, waiting for me to admire him.

"Oh, shut up," I said.

FIXING THE WATER TROUGH

THE AUTOMATIC FLOAT on the horse trough in our middle pasture was leaking. Just a little drip, drip, drip–nothing to worry about, really, and I had cleverly managed to ignore it for a couple of weeks. But this morning was perfect for a fix-it project, blue skies with only a tiny bit of a breeze, so I gathered my tools and headed down there.

It was a Little Giant float, that generic contraption which sits in almost every horse trough in the west. From time to time one of them will spring a leak, and the remedy for that is to take it off, take it apart and put it back together and, magically, it stops leaking. I can't explain it, but that's how it's done. I had a screwdriver, and a pair of channel-lock pliers and a mug of coffee, everything a well-prepared repair guy could possibly need, and I skipped down to the pasture ready to disassemble and reassemble as required.

My dog followed me. He looked worried.

Imagine my pleasure when I realized the leak was coming not from the Little Giant, but from the brass hose bib. The six-foot hose running from the bib to the float needed a new washer, that's all, an even easier fix, and it just so happened I had a brand new one in my shirt pocket. I had thought of everything. I congratulated myself. At this point I dared to whistle a happy little tune, and petted my dog. He still looked more than a little anxious.

I tried unscrewing the hose, but months of sun and rain and rust had welded it solid to the bib, which was screwed into a collar attached to the PVC thingy sticking out of the ground. This was going to take a tool. I unlimbered the channel-locks and applied them to the hose end.

And promptly snapped the bib completely off the collar.

A fountain of water shot high into the air, an arc of silver against the blue sky. You could see little rainbows in it.

The shut-off valve was a couple hundred yards away. I made it in fifteen seconds. I used my outdoor voice to say a few choice words, then went to the barn and brought back a shovel. Still, I wasn't concerned.

"You think this is a problem," I told the dog, "but it's not. It's just a glitch, that's all. I've got it under control."

The dog found a shady spot and laid down in it. He put his chin on his paws and watched me. He sighed, heavily.

I commenced chiseling with the shovel around the PVC thingy. I remembered that it was actually called a riser, not a thingy, though it didn't rise very high anymore. The dirt was soaked down a whole eighth of an inch, and below that the ground was like concrete. The shovel blade bounced off of it, and made a little pinging sound. At one point I thought I saw sparks. I found an empty peach can and dipped a few splashes of water from the trough onto the riser. I let it settle, and dipped some more. I drank the rest of my coffee and waited. All I needed to do was dig far enough to get another PVC collar cemented onto it. I thought I had a new hose bib somewhere, in one of the coffee cans I keep under my work bench, tucked in there with the rusty bolts and screws and wire nuts and bent nails that are so crucial to ranch life. Still an easy fix, no matter what my dog thought about it.

I tested the ground. Not soft enough yet. I dipped more water, then went to the barn and into the tack room, where I started moving stuff around. There was a black rubber bucket in here somewhere full of PVC fittings, all I had to do was find it. There was an extremely important reason I kept it in the tack room, though I can't remember what it was. I found it behind the jug of DuMore fly spray, under a set of fence stretchers, and hauled it out.

I dumped the bucket over and spread the fittings on the floor and fingered through them. When working with this stuff there is an unwritten rule that says the only fitting you won't have in your bucket is the one you actually need. The riser was a half-inch line, and I wanted a half-inch collar with female pipe thread on one end. I found a ¾ inch collar, a one-inch collar, and a chongo two-incher that was impressive but no help; I found a four-way, and three elbows of the proper size, a couple of ball valves I forgot I had, and a 45-degree coupling I didn't even know they made. I also found my can of PVC pipe cement, which had been baking here in the tack room all summer and was now a solid purple ball of petrified goo. It looked as though I'd have to go to town.

I stepped into the kitchen and told my wife I needed parts and had to go to the hardware store. She nodded quietly, as though she'd been expecting it. She didn't lie down with her paws under her muzzle, but she did heave a sigh much the same way my dog had.

I took the dog with me to the Ace Hardware in Reedley, though he seemed reluctant and I had to speak sharply to him before he'd jump in the truck. I stopped at the donut shop and bought a couple of maple bars to help us feel better about the whole thing. He ate his, but acted like it was a terrible chore, and spent more time chewing it than I thought was necessary. He was being overly dramatic.

At the Ace Hardware I was waited on by a nervous man in a red flannel shirt. He had a pair of reading glasses hung around his neck on a piece of string. I told him what I wanted.

"I don't think we have that," he said, but followed me down the aisle where all the stuff was. We both knelt in front of the PVC bins, and pawed through them. He tried to be helpful, and kept handing me things I didn't need. I would hand them back, then he'd hand me something else, smiling hopefully. At one point he offered up the ball-cock assembly for a toilet, which wasn't even close. Finally he said he would go look in the back, and that was the last I saw of him.

I found the pieces the job required, along with a fresh can of cement, and it was only forty or fifty dollars more for the whole mess than I wanted to spend, but I guess it could have been worse. I drove home. The dog refused to look at me.

I returned to discover that in my absence every ounce of water left in the lines had mysteriously backed up and seeped out of the broken riser. My little arid excavation had become a mudhole, and a good-sized one, too. I went to the barn and found my muck boots and put them on. I had to do some serious bailing with the peach can before I could see where to stick the shovel, but at least now it would be easy digging. I drove the shovel into the mud.

And immediately felt the sharp snap as the riser broke loose from whatever it had been attached to down there.

I won't tell you what I said. But it was colorful.

I bailed and shoveled, and bailed some more, and shoveled some more, and eventually had a mudhole about three feet deep and five feet wide. At the bottom of it was a two-inch PVC line with a T-fitting that had some sort of reducer on it, and I knew I wasn't going to find one of those in my rubber bucket.

I tracked mud all the way to the garage. There was a pegboard mounted above the workbench full of tools hanging on pegs with no special order or system. Pipe wrenches hung behind gardening shears and caulking guns obscured the hammers, but eventually I found my rusty hacksaw. The blade had last been changed about the time Jimmy Carter left office. I located some empty cardboard boxes and carried them back with me to the quagmire, where I broke them down and flattened them into the mud, lay down on them and cussed and fumed and cussed some more, and finally managed to cut the T-fitting from the water line. By the time it was over I looked like a little mud man, but I didn't let that slow me down. I climbed into the truck for another thirty-mile round trip and another go at the Ace Hardware. The dog refused to come along this time, and slinked back to the house. I suspect he didn't want to be seen with me, all gummed up the way I was.

The nervous guy with the glasses and flannel shirt winced when he saw me come in. "My God," he said, "what happened to you?" I grunted and thrust the muddy T-fitting at him. He jumped backwards. "*What?*"

"I need one, just like this. The little adapter dealie, too."

"Adapter dealie?"

I pointed. "That."

"I don't think we have any of—"

I made a noise somewhere between a growl and a snort and headed for the PVC aisle. He followed, blinking and twitching, and I squatted at the bins and began rummaging through the merchandise. I handed him things to get them out of my way.

He said, "Maybe I should go look in the back—"

"You're not going anywhere!" I barked. I shoved the fitting at him again. "Find me one of these. Now!"

"You need to calm down a little, mister."

"It's just a little plumbing job!" I said. "It's not supposed to be that hard!"

After an agonizing search that left nearly every fitting they had scattered across the floor, he found me a T. It wasn't exactly the right one, and I'd have to use three different adapters to funnel it down to half-inch, but it would work. The riser would poke up a foot higher than it used to, but I didn't care. I'd hang some kind of *no trespassing* sign on it to keep the horses from bumping into it, or stepping on it.

As I started the truck I realized it was the middle of the afternoon and, except for the maple bars, I hadn't had lunch, but I was too worked up to stop and eat anything. I was focused now, a solid beam of pure determination. A lesser man—or a smarter one—would shrink in the face of such adversity, throw up his hands and admit defeat, and call a plumber. Not me. No, sir. I wasn't going to let this job whip me. I was going to win, by God, no matter how long it took. Or what it cost.

Back at the ranch (yes, I know; I could have gone all day without saying that), the three horses who lived in the pasture had discovered my project, and were now clustered around the water trough, stomping on the cardboard and poking their noses into everything, trying to figure out what I was up to. They had knocked the pliers and the hacksaw into the mud, and pooped on them. I fished the tools out and laid them aside to dry. I shooed the horses away and jumped back in the foxhole.

The tricky part in a job like this is when you have to get two sections of pipe that used to be one section of pipe back into one section of pipe again. You daub a glob of purple cement onto the west end of the two-inch line and fit the new T-fitting on there, reach into the mudhole and work the east end of the two-inch line into the east end of the fitting, all the while making sure the little adapter dealies are poking up in the proper direction so you can get water to your Little Giant float. To accomplish this, you must squinch your mouth over to one side of your face, like this, with your tongue sticking out. And close one eye, too. I got the west end of the line stuck in there all right, but the other end of the pipe wouldn't flex enough to make the journey. This was the good, heavy PVC, schedule 80, not that flimsy schedule 40 stuff that wobbles around like a rubber hose. This would require some grunting to get into position.

I squatted over the pipe in my rubber muck boots, reached down with both hands and gave it a mighty heave.

And felt, somewhere underground, far down the line, something break.

You know the dreaded feeling. Things have gone terribly wrong, and you're out here all alone. Or maybe you don't know it, and if you don't I hope you never do—though I would have given a hundred bucks to change places with you right then. I heard a pitiful whining noise, and looked around for the dog, then realized it was coming from me.

I think I said, "Are you kidding me?" fourteen times in a row as I walked around and around in a circle. I threw my cap on the ground and yanked at my hair, but there's not enough left on my head to do any good so I quit that, and instead stumbled to my John Deere tractor and fired it up. I wheeled her around and in through the gate.

By dusk I had used the front bucket to scrape out a twenty-foot ditch that was five feet wide and two feet deep, and still hadn't found the pipe. It was down there somewhere. Hiding from me. The horses were huddled together at the far end of the pasture, cowering in fear. I knew I had been making noises while I worked, hollering and cussing and laughing maniacally, but I doubted they could hear me over the roar of the engine. I don't know what their deal was. Horses are too sensitive sometimes. The ground was hard, and getting harder the deeper I went, and the thought came to me that I didn't know where the break was, exactly, but if I turned the water back on I could find out. I think I said, "Ah *hah*!" but I can't be sure. I probably did. When I get into these situations I tend to say that a lot. It never seems to do any good, but I still say it.

I had to stop at the house and collect a flashlight. My wife was at the counter with her laptop, doing some bookwork, the dog on the floor at her feet. The dog glowered when I came in. My wife looked at me, at all the crusted mud and at my red eyes. "My God!" she said. "What happened to you?"

"Almost there!" I said.

"You do realize you've had the water turned off all day, don't you?"

"I'm turning it back on right now."

"Good, because I have to—"

"But only for a minute."

"What?"

"Almost there! Don't worry!"

I scuttled off before she could ask more pesky questions.

With my trusty flashlight in hand I went to the shut off valve, cranked it open, and proceeded to the pasture to wait developments. The water, I calculated, would burble up from the broken pipe, come to the surface and make a little mudhole. When that happened I'd quickly shut the water off again, return with my shovel and start digging where the new mudhole was. This was my brilliant plan.

It was dark now, and getting darker. As I reached the pasture I heard a strange noise—a rumbling, boiling sound, such as a river might make when it leaves its bed and crashes through a boulder-strewn canyon where it isn't supposed to go. A torrential sound. I played the flashlight beam across the pasture and it reflected back from a geyser of water shooting fifteen feet into the air.

"Uh-oh," I said.

I headed, once more, for the shut-off.

It was a big, two-inch ball valve with a red handle. I don't know how old it was, but I had a vague notion I'd replaced it not that long ago. A couple years, maybe. I could hear the water hissing through it as I grabbed the red handle and gave it a yank.

It came off in my hand.

An icy spray hit me in the face and knocked my glasses into the darkness. Along with my cap. I ripped my shirt off and wrapped it around the valve. I don't know why. I thought it might help. It didn't. The shirt soaked through in seconds and the icy spray continued. The little Dutch boy at the dike had nothing on me.

My only chance was to head for the pressure tank and shut the pump down, and that was way the hell and gone on the other side of the property. It's hard to run when you are over sixty, and wearing rubber muck boots, but I made it just in time to smell the burning electrical wires in the control box and hear the pump motor strain and slow and quit completely just as I reached for the switch.

It had been a good pump. Very efficient. It took no time at all for a pump that good to suck every drop of water out of the well, and then they don't run so good after that.

In the end, I think it cost around fifteen hundred bucks to pull and replace it.

It took me almost a week to fill in the ditch and the yawning crevice carved out by the geyser. My wife called a plumber from town to come repair the PVC line and put the horse trough back together. She never told me how much it cost, but I'm no longer allowed to tinker with anything that has water running through it. Period. And I'm okay with that, mostly.

The faucet in our bathroom, however, has started leaking a little. Just a drip, drip drip, nothing major. It kinda bothers me.

COYOTES AND
MUSICIANS

THE COYOTES ARE doing their best to drive my dogs crazy. And I think they're succeeding, with one of them, at least. She's not a very bright dog. I think the coyotes know this, and are having fun with her. They gather in the middle of the night just the other side of the fence, frolicking and yapping, until she comes out to bark at them, and then they run up and down the fence taunting her, laughing at her, calling her names and making rude comments about her stubby little tail and goodness knows what all else. Coyotes are vicious with an insult. The dog chases up and down the fenceline after them, barking her head off. This goes on for better than an hour, often several times a night, and while it provides plenty of exercise for the dog, it tends to startle me out of bed and makes me say bad words out loud. Eventually I stomp outside, barefooted in my bathrobe, carrying a .410 shotgun. I let off a couple of blasts into the air, and it disperses them—temporarily, anyway. The dog quits barking and goes back to bed. She has no trouble falling right to sleep, while I always end up laying there for two or three hours, twitching and fuming.

Our other dog, who is older and smarter, and more world-weary, recognizes these varmints for the immature trouble-makers they are, and ignores them. I believe he's tried to convince the female that all this barking and scurrying around only encourages them, but he's given up now. There's no talking to her. All it takes is one coyote to yip and wail, and her head disappears right up her hind end and she's off and running.

The coyote population around our place has exploded the last few years. There will be a dozen of them crouched among the rocks on the hill back of our house, wailing and howling, and pretty quick they'll set off another pack across the valley who will join in with their yipping and yapping, and this will set off yet another bunch in the trees behind the turkey farm, and suddenly it sounds like a thousand of them have descended upon us, crazed and slobbering. Yet none of them seem interested in doing the one job I'd like them to do—their actual, normal job, which is killing and eating all the ground squirrels.

The ground squirrels are everywhere, and I mean every damn where. They excavate through my wife's rose garden. They burrow up into the barn to get at the chicken scratch. They crawl into the engine compartment of my pickup to gnaw on the electrical wiring. They are fat and sleek, and swarm carefree through the dried grass under the oak trees by the hundreds, and you'd think a coyote would find them irresistible and delicious-looking, but are they interested? Any of them? The answer seems to be no. Perhaps they've signed some sort of non-aggression treaty. If they have, it hasn't done the coyote faction any good, because they still look scrawny and hungry. But then again, they always do.

Coyotes are lazy by nature. If you were to shoot a ground squirrel and throw it over the fence, they'd happily eat it, but to actually chase one down and kill it is too much bother. I've never met a coyote who was burning up with ambition. As long as they've got a few bucks in their pockets they don't worry about tomorrow, or next month, or how they'll spend their retirement years. They lay in bed until noon, then stumble around with their hair sticking up all over the place, hoping somebody's already made the coffee so they don't have to; then somehow they manage to scrounge up enough to eat, and when they're done with that they torment my dogs. It's a pretty simple life, similar in many ways to being a musician.

There are a number of parallels. Both coyotes and musicians are opportunistic, and we both make noise after the sun goes down. Not everybody likes our music. While the noises I make have yet to produce a critic in a bathrobe carrying a shotgun, at least not yet, there have been incidents. One evening at a bar in Paso Robles a slope-browed Neandertal threatened to pinch my little head off—his exact words—if I couldn't come up with some songs he wanted to hear. Like the cowardly coyote, musicians have the magical ability to vanish into the shadows when danger rears its head. I skulked off into the parking lot and smoked cigarettes until the ugly man passed out at his table, which he did not long after.

We both keep weird hours, which is just another way of hiding from the world. When you are eating thin bacon and runny eggs in a Denny's restaurant at three in the morning after the gig, you don't have to worry about Mr. Finster from the bank calling you to discuss your latest overdraft. The credit card people seldom hound you at that hour about missed payments. Nobody bothers you. The people who inhabit Denny's at three in the morning, the creepy people, the sick and lame, unshaven, with their haunted eyes and sunken cheeks, don't even want to glance up from their coffee cups, let alone bother anyone. You are in an insulated bubble of safety that will last until business hours tomorrow, and you're going to sleep through most of those, anyway. And every musician knows, as does the coyote, that a sunrise is a really cool thing to look at just before you go to bed.

We both tend to shy away from responsibility—to avoid it completely, if at all possible. The coyotes actually have it easier here. I've mentioned their failings when it comes to the ground squirrel problem; but people just say, well, they're coyotes, what can you expect? They get a pass. Musicians, however, are looked universally down upon, showered with constant disapproval and even contempt. It's enough to give you a complex. The neighbors frown and shake their heads. They keep their blinds drawn when you're at home, and call the cops if you rehearse too loudly. They've given up wondering if you'll ever get a real job, and now just hope their daughter won't want to date you. They see the artistic temperament as an excuse to flit around without form or plan, trying to make it across town on an eighth of a tank of gas and, oh, by the way, your tags have expired. When will you let go of this tattered fantasy and apply yourself to something realistic and achievable and respectable? Why is your hair so long, and why are your pets so skinny?

And yes, from time to time we can both look a bit scruffy. Our appearance is not some angry statement against the status quo, by the way. You need to be interested in the rest of the world to make that kind of statement, and most musicians are not. Musicians are notoriously self-absorbed. It's just that the fifteen bucks we might have given to the barber to cut our hair seemed better spent on beer and guitar picks, or the overdue phone bill, or even a jar of chunky peanut butter and a loaf of Wonder Bread—the fallback cuisine of every musician who ever picked up a guitar.

I guess that's why I never actually shoot at the coyotes around our place. Making loud noises to scare them off is one thing, but when I actually catch sight of them, with their raggedy pelts and every rib showing, their frantic, malnourished expressions, I'm reminded of all the bass players I ever worked with. They could never keep a regular job, either. I doubt any of them were ever hired to muck out ground squirrels, but they had a hard enough time hanging in there at the convenience store, or the car wash. I still have sympathy for bass players. That sympathy leaks over to the coyote population.

My dog has an issue with them, however. With the coyotes, not the bass players. They're driving her crazy.

THE SILAGE PIT

I WAS A puzzlement to my father. He was a man's man, a southerner who came to Montana with the ungainly dream of becoming a rancher. He knew how to work on trucks and cars and tractors, and liked being outside, where he could hunt and fish, and kill things. I, on the other hand, was a quiet kid. I liked to read books, and draw pictures and listen to records, and daydream, and this deeply, deeply worried him. I think he was afraid I'd turn into a sissy, and embarrass him.

"You been reading on them books again, ain't you, boy?" he'd say. "Get off your ass and come outside and help me. I need you to hold the flashlight while I pull the water pump off that truck."

He did a lot of this stuff after dark, mostly because he had to work in town every day to keep the ranch afloat, since his agricultural adventures didn't pay very well. Every piece of equipment on the place was ancient and clanking and unreliable, which meant that many repairs took place under the star-lit sky, which meant that someone had to hold the flashlight for him—a horrifying job, a dreadful job, a job that always ended up being mine. And I could never seem to do it right.

I was supposed to automatically know which bolt or nut or plug wire he needed to look at next, and I never had the slightest clue. I'd shine the light on the carburetor, or the distributor, or in his eyes, every spot but the right one, and he'd squint at me through his cigarette smoke and growl and cuss and let me know what a lousy job I was doing.

"Jesus Christ, boy, use your head for something besides a hat rack, why don't you?"

At the end of these agonies he would stomp back to the house and describe for anyone who wanted to listen just how short of expectations, once again, I had fallen.

"Like working with a half-wit. I believe the goddamn dog could hold the light in his mouth and do a better job."

The one person always eager to listen, of course, was my younger brother Danny. An evil child whose sole purpose on earth was to make my life a living hell, Danny never had to do any of these rotten jobs, because he played football, and this made him perfect in my father's eyes, and exempted him from trouble and care. I wasn't a football player, and this was an aberration that screamed to be corrected. Maybe, if my flaws were constantly pointed out, and my failings publicly aired enough times for my own good, I would change and become an athlete, and make the old man proud. My brother thought this was a good plan, and joined in, listening to every critique with glee, carefully cataloging the best zingers in his head so he could trot them out again and repeat them over and over, with gusto, in case I'd missed them the first time around, or forgotten them.

"Dad doesn't even like you very much," he tittered. "You're a disgrace to our father. You don't play football because you're scared of getting hurt. You're just a big pansy." And so on.

I wasn't all that scared, particularly. I just didn't see the point of getting bashed around for no reason. Animals bashed me around all the time, and I wasn't afraid of them. Pigs ran over me, big pigs, sows and half-grown gilts and barrows who didn't want to go where I was trying to haze them; calves ran over me at brandings, even the cute little ones you wouldn't think could do that, weak and runty calves; and one of our grouchy old horses had scraped me off against a tree a couple of times. Okay, a bunch of times. I wasn't scared, but I didn't care for it very much. Playing football, it seemed to me, was by definition going out to look for such abuse on purpose. Why do that? It was crazy.

"Will James never played football," I'd say, invoking the name of a local hero, "and he turned out all right. And Jesus never played football."

"Jesus would have too played football, if they'd only invented it then."

"There's nothing in the Bible about football."

"Jesus woulda been a great football player. He'd of been a wide receiver."

"Wouldn't he be the quarterback?"

Danny thought about it. You had to be careful what you said about Jesus around our house. You could get slapped. "I guess so, yeah. But *you* couldn't. You wouldn't make a pimple on a quarterback's rump, because you're a pansy."

And so it went.

At some point many years back, a previous owner had run a bunch of dairy cows on our place. Like countless other desperate rural endeavors whipped to the four winds, the milk cows were long gone, along with whatever dreams the dairyman had harbored; but behind the barn, out past the haystacks, was a pit still half full of corn silage. Silage was a common cattle feed in that part of Yellowstone County—feed-corn country. Like all silage pits, ours was covered with black plastic sheeting, the kind that came in big rolls from the Western Auto store in Billings. This sheeting was, of course, anchored down by old tires. You had to have old tires on your black plastic, it was just part of the deal. I think it was in fact a Montana state law at the time: All silage must be covered with black plastic and held down by old tires, world without end, God bless America.

At the bottom of the pit, where the silage had been scooped out, were more old tires, slick tractor tires and skinny old-fashioned truck tires, the rusted sickle bar off an ancient hay mow, the links and gears from a wrecked manure spreader, and other shards of discarded farm equipment, all of them jagged and sharp and dripping with tetanus. It was a pretty dangerous place, now that I think of it, and as kids we were down there playing around in it every chance we got.

One day, out at the silage pit, I said, "You know, you could get drunk off this stuff."

Danny squinched up his face, something between a sneer and the expression you make after smelling something rancid. It was his standard reaction to anything I ever said. "No, you couldn't."

"It's fermented, ain't it?"

"What's that mean?"

"It's how they make alcohol, and whiskey and stuff. They ferment it, and it gets you drunk."

I went on to tell him the story about some pigs a guy had, how they fed these pigs fermented silage and the pigs got drunk and stumbled around, and walked sideways into their feed troughs and fell down, a hilarious scene anybody would enjoy watching, given the chance. I think I'd heard about it somewhere, or maybe I just made it up, I don't remember. It was a good story, though. I was pleased with it when I was done.

"Could it get a cow drunk?" Danny asked.

"I'm not sure. I don't think so."

"How come?"

"Because a cow's got two or three stomachs, something like that."

Again with the squinched-up face. "No, they don't."

"Yes, they do. And I think if you have more than one stomach you can't get drunk."

"Really?"

I nodded sagely. I had no idea if this was the case or not, but it sounded good, and I was two years older and could at least act like I knew more than he did. Mr. Bunch, one of the teachers at school, had told me about a cow having multiple stomachs, so that part was true enough.

We scurried to the mound of silage and started excavating around. I had it in my head you needed to find the warmest spot in the pile, because that was where the action was, all that chemical stuff bubbling along, turning corn juice into nitro. It was a warm summer day, so the black plastic sheeting was sure hot enough, nearly to the point where it turned into molten lava. The silage underneath seemed cool in comparison. There was a winey, sour smell to it, like a nasty black banana you left in your fruit bowl too long, with all those little flies buzzing around it. Undaunted, we dug on.

I found a juicy piece of corn stalk, about three inches long. It had a gray, greenish color. I poked it at Danny, hoping to see him reeling around and walking sideways as soon as possible. "Here, try it."

"I ain't putting that in my mouth."

"Go ahead. It'll be great."

"You first."

Well. We'd gone to all this trouble, I couldn't very well back out now. I bit down on it gingerly, using only the teeniest edges of my front teeth. The corn stalk, an ancient artifact that had lain under that plastic sheeting for probably better than thirty years, was nasty. It tasted like an evil leprechaun had snuck up and peed in my mouth. I spit it out immediately, then picked it up again and shoved it toward Danny.

"Get away from me," he said.

"No, really, it's not that bad."

"How come you spit it out, then?"

"I thought there was a bug."

"You're such a dork."

"What're you, scared?"

Those were the magic words. Danny wasn't scared of a single thing in the whole wide world, except our old man, and he'd fight anyone who said otherwise, me especially. He grabbed the piece of corn stalk and chomped down on it, and immediately began spitting and hacking and cursing, and called me every nasty name he could think of, and almost threw up right there, which would have been wonderful, except he didn't.

I recalled how the old man often bragged of his ancestors back in North Carolina, barefoot men with long beards who skulked about the southern mountains, making moonshine and running away from the Revenuers—our own personal heritage—and all I could think was, if the liquor they distilled was anything like this, they had to be the stupidest people who ever lived.

"What about chickens?" Danny said.

"What about them?"

"Could you get them drunk?"

It was worth a try. We gathered a couple double-handfuls of silage and ran to the chicken house to spread them around and await developments. It was close and stuffy in there and smelled of feathers and chicken poop. A pair of Leghorn hens wandered over and pecked absently at the stuff, then wandered off again. Chickens, notoriously brainless, were apparently smarter than we were.

I think it was a few days later that Steve and Debbie Tate came over. They were neighbor kids from a mile or so down the gravel road, and their father and ours had been in the Marine Corps together, in Korea and were sort of best friends. Steve was a year younger than me, a wiry kid with a wild shock of yellow hair, and his sister Debbie was my age, a head taller and at least fifteen pounds heavier than me. She was getting boobs, which was interesting, and she had a crush on me, but I didn't know what to do about it. She would sidle up and whisper, "You know, I really dig you," and then punch me in the arm and run off. Once she hit me so hard it left a big purple bruise that took a couple weeks to fade, and I decided if this was romance I wanted no part of it.

Of course we wound up at the silage pit, as usual. We always wound up there—it was like a black hole, throbbing with irresistible gravity, sucking us in, hungry and insistent.

"I know what let's do," Steve said.

He clambered to the bottom and dragged up a pair of old car tires. He set one of them on edge in front of him and, closing one eye to sight in his target, kicked the tire back down. We watched as it bounced and wobbled and came to rest in a puff of dust.

"Well, that's kinda stupid," Danny said, always ready with a dismissive sneer whenever it could be inserted.

"Naw, it ain't," Steve said. "Watch."

He kicked the second tire into action. This one rolled like a scalded rabbit, all the way through the garbage at the bottom of the pit and a quarter of the way up the other side.

"See how far that one went? I wonder could we get one all the way to the top over there—if we could make it roll fast enough."

It was a dandy idea, a stellar idea. All four of us went to work like a bunch of little service station attendants, grunting up and down the slope, hauling tires to the top and stacking them in piles, ready to go. We took turns kicking them back down, cheering when a new record was made up the opposite bank, and groaning when a tire failed us and only wobbled anemically to the bottom. Every so often one would bounce off another on the way down and soar high into the air, an exciting development, and everybody shouted their approval. Once, I was on the other side with a stick, marking the heights of previous attempts, when a Goodyear bias-ply did a wild bounce against a tractor tire and nearly took my head off. Only by performing an artful dodge and pirouette at the last second did I save myself. I tumbled partway down the slope, but managed to walk away with only a bunch of dirt down my underwear. Everybody shouted their approval then, too, but I knew what they were happy about was how close I'd come to being flattened.

"Jeez, you guys."

Debbie clumped over, looking all doe-eyed and concerned. "Are you okay?" she asked, reaching out a paw. I cringed away, because she sounded a little girlish right then, and I didn't feel like getting teased by Danny and Steve, which would happen for sure if she actually touched me, even by accident. They'd pile on me like wild dogs.

"I'm fine, leave me alone," I said.

"Sure," she said, and then slugged me. Pretty hard. I fell down, but got up again right away.

As great as this game was, we got bored with it after about a half hour, and started poking around for something more adventurous and exciting to do—maybe even death-defying. In our little world, any activity that did not bring with it the risk of getting killed, or at least badly maimed and disfigured, seemed bland and uninteresting.

I hate to admit it, but I'm pretty sure it was me who thought of it. The amazing part was how everybody else thought it was brilliant, and wanted to try it. The first was Steve, who was always ready and eager to cheat death.

Once again we toted a slew of tires up the slope.

Steve said, "Wait, let me find the best spot. Here—over here. There's kind of a steep drop-off. Yeah, this is good."

He stood still, waiting, grinning like a baboon with his arms held flat to his sides. Danny was too short, so it was Debbie and I who had to lift the tires into position and drop them over Steve's noggin. He was skinny as a whip, like we all were in those days, so it was easy to stack the tires up. Pretty soon all you could see was his yellow head.

"Shouldn't you stick your hands up to protect your face?" I asked.

"Naw, it'll be great."

"You ready?"

"How're you gonna do it?"

"I dunno. Just shove you over and roll you down, I guess. You ready?"

"Yeah. Stack the last tire on."

There were a number of holes in this plan. They never occurred to any of us. We simply assumed that tires, being made of rubber would, naturally, both bounce and protect the passenger, all at the same time. We were really dumb.

"Okay. On three. One, two—THREE!"

I shoved. Steve teetered, but would not go over.

"One, two—THREE!"

This time, here came Debbie to add her substantial oomph, and Steve went down like a dead cottonwood in a high wind, letting out a weird squawking noise as he tilted over the edge. He struck a dirt ledge a quarter of the way down. Tires went flying off at both ends, and he made another noise, a higher, squeakier noise— "*Aaaack!*"—and whanged off that same tractor tire and went airborne, to land in a cloud of dirt and silage and rusty nails and T-posts at the bottom of the pit. There were only two tires left around his middle.

He lay dishrag limp for quite some time. We watched, hawk-like, for any sort of movement, a twitch or a shudder, even a spasm, that would tell us he was still alive. Eventually, a finger wiggled. Then a leg. He sat up.

"Man! That was wild!"

There wasn't as much blood as you might expect. He had a cut on his cheek, and a red welt across his forehead, and his arms were skinned up, but otherwise he seemed intact.

"How was it?" I asked.

"A little rough. You kinda feel all floppy in there."

"Floppy?"

"You know, it bounces you around. You'll see. Try it!"

I discovered that I was a little less excited about joining in the festivities than I had been only moments before, replaying in my head the huge bounce Steve took just before he landed. Also the cut on his cheek was starting to bleed in earnest, and his skinned-up arms looked sort of painful. Still, it was time to put-up or shut-up. There was no way I could back down with my evil brother standing there, frothing at the mouth, waiting for just such a move so that he could hold it over my head for years and years to come.

We went to hauling tires again. My legs felt heavy as I toted a couple of recaps back to the top of the pit. My shoes weighed a hundred pounds each, and my arms were suddenly weak and shaky. Danny danced around me, cackling gleefully and pointing a stubby finger, saying, "You're going to chicken out, ain't you? You're going to be a pansy and chicken out, you're such a dork, just a big chicken, cluck-cluck-cluck!"

Debbie said, "I'm not sure I wanna do it, either."

Anny said, "You can bet *he* won't, the big wussy. He's gonna go sit in the chicken house with the hens. Cluck-cluck-cluck!" He waggled his elbows up and down like a pair of little boney wings.

They had to stack five tires on top of me before I was completely covered up. They smelled of nasty old rubber and mildew and dirt, and I just knew there were spiders in there with me, big gnarly spiders with furry fangs and hairy legs. Danny frolicked around me, almost desperately, saying, "You're gonna die now, you're gonna break both arms and maybe your legs, too, gonna die, gonna die, gonna die. . ."

"Naw, he ain't," Steve said. "He'll be fine."

Finally we were ready. Or at least everybody else was, anxious to watch me crash and burn. I could have stood there a year and still not been ready.

"Okay, here we go," Steve said. "Debbie, come help me shove him over. On the count of three. One, two—"

"Wait! I need to move my hands up—"

"THREE!"

Over I went, and I was tumbling. A dice in a cup, a pea in a barrel, helpless, all ten of those tire beads biting and battering me at the same time, the tire around my head whacking me a savage blow before it went careening off into the atmosphere. I think I made noises, I don't remember, all at once I was at the bottom with every ounce of air pummeled from my body and the dust settling around me, the way it does after a car crash.

Debbie called, "Are you okay?"

Uh-oh. I was scared she might come down here, and touch me. I tried to suck in a breath to say something, but my lungs were flattened.

"*Eeeeee*," I explained.

"He's all right," Steve said.

I looked at the sky, the cool blue, cloudless sky, the last thing I would ever see. I waited for death, knowing I would never breathe again. This was the stupidest day of my life. I could feel my lower lip swelling up, and my right eye trying to close. I took a hesitant inventory and nothing seemed broken, nothing important, anyway, but you never could tell about that. Maybe I was in shock, and the pain from all these internal injuries would start later. I'd heard of such things happening.

Eventually breath and life returned to my body. I managed to peel myself out of the wreckage. There was a huge rip in the left leg of my jeans, and my shirt looked like it had been pooped on by a vicious tire monster. I crawled to the top of the slope.

"You screamed," Danny said, smugly.

"I did not."

"Yes, you did. You did so. You screamed like a little girl. You went, 'Aaaaaaagh!'"

"Shut up. I didn't, neither."

"You're bleeding," Debbie said.

"Just a little," Steve said.

I wiped a hand across my face, and discovered a split lip.

"I ain't doing this," Debbie said.

Danny was frantic to be the next one to get hurled down the hill, and right now, please. No way could he allow me to walk away with the upper hand. I had done it, and now he by God had to do it, too.

"And I'll do it better than you did," he sneered.

"Do what better?"

"I won't just lay there, sniveling, like you. I'll jump right up, you watch and see."

"I never sniveled," I said.

"You did so. You sniveled all over the place. But I won't, because I'm tougher than you."

It only took four tires to get him covered. We pushed him over and kicked him down the slope, with me giving an extra little boot at the last second, and he landed in a predictably tangled mess at the bottom, where he lay crying. This gave me a proud moment. But then he kept on crying, and I was scared he'd really hurt himself and I'd be held responsible. I was the older brother, I was supposed to know better, whatever that meant. The only thing it ever meant was that I was the one who got in trouble.

It turns out he was only shaken up.

"I thought you were going to leap to your feet," I said.

"Shut up, pansy."

"You didn't leap to your feet. I think you were sniveling."

"I wasn't, either."

"You were crying. Everybody heard you."

"I just got the wind knocked out of me."

That evening, at supper, the old man looked at the pair of us and asked if we'd been fighting again. I had a black eye and a busted lip, and Danny was covered with an assortment of scrapes and contusions. We were known to thump each other on a regular basis, so it was a reasonable question. Danny described our afternoon adventure, and how brave he, especially, had been riding the black tire monster down the hill.

"Did you try it, too?" the old man asked me.

"I went first," I said, proudly.

Danny said, "He didn't do it very good, though."

The old man rolled his eyes at our mother. "You boys stay out of that pit. You're lucky you didn't break your necks."

After supper the old man directed me to get my jacket and flashlight and follow him outside. He had to change the oil in the Allis Chalmers and my marginal skills as a light-shiner were needed. At the tool shed beside the barn he loaded me down with wrenches and sockets and breaker bars and drip pan, and led the way to the tractor, where he donned coveralls and crawled underneath.

"Hand me that pan. No, take the tools out of it first, Einstein." He fussed and grunted and cursed, and asked for the breaker bar.

"Shine your light right here. Not there, over here—look at where my finger is. Right here."

I squatted with my flashlight. Heaved a sigh. It was going to be a long night.

"So," he said. "Tell me again how come you don't want to play football. Explain it to me. You scared, is that it? A scaredy-cat?"

I shrugged, and fell silent, the only defense I had left. There was no point in protesting, or arguing, or sniveling. If I could brave the dangers of the silage pit and still be accused of cowardice, my situation was hopeless.

"No," he said, "get the light out of my eyes. Damn it, boy, I can't see."

DONNY & YOLANDA

I T WAS ONE of those moments you look back and always remember, like the first time you got bucked off, or touched a girl's boobie, or when you heard Elvis had died.

Sam said, "What do you mean, getting married? To who?"

We were in the tack room. We'd finished saddling the horses and had a few minutes before the dudes started showing up at the front gate. Ray was sprawled in a rusty folding chair, leafing through an ancient *Western Horseman,* and Mark was leaning against the file cabinet, putting a new Chicago screw into a bridle with a screwdriver that was too big for the job. I was at the dented green percolator dribbling out a cup of coffee. It was terrible coffee, as usual. Just nasty. Donny made the coffee every day and nobody could figure out what he did to it to make it taste so bad. It was like he used metal shavings and stagnant pond water. There just wasn't any reason for it. We called it *Depresso.*

Everything went quiet. Everybody stared.

"T-t-to a lady I met," Donny said.

Donny tended to stutter when he got excited. His eyes would blink really fast, and he'd sort of twitch all over with the effort of getting the words out. It could put people off if you didn't know him, but we were all used to it.

"Met where?" Sam said.

"On the internet," Donny said.

Lisa came in carrying an armload of wet cinches she'd just cleaned at the hose bib out back. There was a concrete slab out there we used for shoeing horses and washing saddle pads and feed buckets, and Lisa, who had a ridiculously tireless work ethic, was always fussing around with such chores. She liked working on the concrete because she could use the hose and not get her boots muddy. Tall and thin-hipped and wind-burned, her hair in a thick blond braid that hung down her back, she was kind of cute in a Western, outdoorsy way. But you didn't want to mess with her, because she could whip your ass.

"What's going on?" she asked.

"Donny says he's getting married," Ray smirked, dropping his magazine. "To a girl he met on his computer. Hey, Donny, she ain't one of them Russian gals you hear about, is she?"

"Just never mind, Ray," Donny sputtered. His face, already glowing, turned even redder. "She's from San Diego. Down there by San Diego somewhere."

We all stood there, trying to digest this news, with stunned expressions on our faces. I assume my expression was stunned. Everybody else's sure were.

Donny was pushing sixty, and lived in a cramped room in the bunkhouse. It was a dark, airless little warren equipped with a hotplate, on which he cooked his meals of Chef Boyardee Ravioli, or baked beans with cut-up hotdogs. He had a bed in there, and a little television and a refrigerator, and it was whispered that his shower had never been used, a whisper you had no trouble believing once the hot weather came and you stood too close to him. When he wasn't working he stayed caved up in that room, seldom poking his grizzled muzzle out the door except to drive to the post office, or maybe to Ellen's Pancake House once in a while for breakfast. You could hear that television blaring every night. It made no sense that he could journey all the way to San Diego without one of us knowing about it, let alone spend enough time down there to find somebody who wanted to marry him.

Sam said, "Wait a minute. You don't even know where she lives?"

"Yeah," Donny said, "I do. Sort of."

"Sort of? Either you know or you don't. Where did you meet her when you met her?"

"Well," Donny waffled, "I talked to her on the phone."

"On the phone."

"Yeah. A couple of times."

Sam took off his hat and rubbed a hand across his buzzed scalp and put the hat back on again. "My God, you're serious, aren't you?"

Donny just stared back at him, as if having such a discussion was the most normal thing in the world. Mark, still carrying the broken bridle, shook his head and walked outside to check on the horses. Mark never said much.

The wet cinches Lisa held were dripping on the floor. She looked around for something to do with them, and finally laid them across an empty saddle rack. "Donny, how much do you really know about this— what's her name?"

"Yolanda."

"Yolanda. What do you know about this Yolanda person?"

Ray said, "I bet she could be an axe murderer, huh?"

Donny said, "Shut up, Ray. She's a nice lady."

"How do you know?" Lisa said. "You've never even seen her, have you?"

"She sent me her picture," Donny said.

Ray said, "Was she naked?"

Sam had been sitting at the old wooden desk, making notes on some paperwork with a golf pencil. Now he gathered the papers into a loose stack. "This is weird. This is way, *way* too weird." He got up and wandered out, heading for the front office.

Lisa said, "Shouldn't you at least go on a couple of dates before you decide to get married? Wouldn't it be smarter to get to know each other a little?"

"She's pretty excited about it. She says we should go to Las Vegas and get married there."

"So you really asked her? You really proposed?"

"She asked me," Donny said, proudly.

"Did you send her a picture?" Ray asked.

"Course I did," Donny said.

"Was it a recent one? Or did you send her a picture when you were nineteen and still had your hair?"

"It was a new picture."

"And she still wants to marry you?"

Donny just clammed up, his usual strategy when Ray got to picking on him, which was pretty much all the time. He scuttled over to Sam's desk and gathered a fresh handful of liability waivers, clamped them to his clipboard and headed for the gate. A cluster of guests were already waiting there, peering anxiously this way, eager to climb onto an innocent dude horse and lope off into the sunset.

Ray, watching him go, said, "I'll be dipped. That's the most hilarious thing I ever heard."

Lisa looked at me. "What are we gonna do?"

"Do?" I said. "I don't know. I don't know if there's anything we can do. Donny's a growed man. Been growed for quite a while."

"I'll bet she's one of those predators. I've heard about people like that, people who troll on the computer looking for victims. Like a vampire or something."

I said she might be right, this Yolanda lady could be a predator, but not a very smart one if she figured Donny for a good prospect. It wasn't like he was a millionaire with bags of cash laying around. He was just a little weenie dude wrangler in run-down boots and a crumply straw cowboy hat.

"It's the little people like Donny who always get hurt," Lisa said. "We should do something. Before it's too late."

"Aw," Ray said, "ten bucks says it don't ever happen. She'll take one look at him and run like a rabbit. You watch."

Turns out Ray's prognostications were about as wrong as they could be. A week or so after Donny's announcement, first thing on a Wednesday morning, Lisa darted up to me as I stepped into the tack room. I hadn't even made it to the coffee pot yet.

"She's here."

"Huh?"

"And it's creepy."

"What's creepy?"

"Donny and Yolanda. She's *here.*"

And so she was, out in the saddling corral, hanging onto Donny's arm, big as life. Or almost big as life. There wasn't much to her.

You know how sometimes you see a little old couple married for so long they've started to look like each other? Well, Donny and Yolanda were already there. Just dinky things, the two of them, side by side, like little stick people, or salt and pepper shakers. Of course, Donny had a mustache and Yolanda didn't, but even so they could have been brother and sister they were so much alike, both wearing thick eyeglasses, both looking mousy and intense, both moving with exaggerated slowness, a kind of solemnity, around the corral, first to this wrangler and then to that one, as Donny introduced her to the crew. Yolanda smiled a lot, but she was so pinched up it looked painful, the way a heeler dog looks when it grins at you, all hunkered down and showing pointy little teeth. Not that Yolanda's teeth were pointy. At least not as far as I could tell.

Sam had fled to the shoeing slab, where he could put his head down and be busy and not have to pay attention to all this. He was hunched under a big sorrel gelding named Mickey, hind foot in his lap, nailing on a #1 St. Croix when the happy couple arrived to stand, expectantly, before him.

Donny waited until the nails were driven and the ends twisted off, and then, red-faced and stuttering like he'd let his clutch out too fast, managed an introduction. Sam set the hoof down and straightened up, moved the shoeing hammer to his left hand and, daintily so as not to get hoof-crud on her, shook the tips of Yolanda's fingers.

"Yolanda, it's good to meet you. How you doing?"

Yolanda smiled her tight little smile and wiped her fingers down the leg of her pantsuit. She nodded, her brillo-pad hair bouncing in the front.

"It's a pleasure to meet *you*, Sam," she said. She had a small, needly voice, almost as nasal as Donny's. It was spooky, how matched they were. "Donald speaks of you all the time, talking about what a great boss you are. He hardly talks about anything else, in fact, he just goes on and on about you."

Donny said, "aw, honey. . ."

Lisa whispered, "Good God. He calls her *honey*. I'm going to throw up."

Sam cast his eyes quickly left and right, as if looking for some kind of help, or hoping that something else would happen so this could be over. "Well, we sure couldn't run this place without Donny, that's for sure."

"Yes. He says that, too."

Sam's eyebrows bounced in surprise, like she'd poked him with a finger. He scowled, and looked around again. "People! Aren't there horses that need saddling?"

It wasn't too awful busy this morning, but a couple of wranglers oozed off toward the catch pen. Donny, still gallant and attentive, led Yolanda around to the rest of us, but after meeting Sam she didn't bother talking much. She'd say hello, and barely meet your eyes, then tuck her head in that cowed puppy dog fashion and move on to the next subject in the receiving line. I noticed she was wearing leather wrist braces, the kind that people use who have Carpal Tunnel troubles, and I asked her about them when she got to me. Just trying to make conversation—some people like talking about their aches and pains.

"She used to be a policeman," Donny said. "She hurt herself when she was, you know, chasing a robber."

Yolanda said, "And I fell off a ladder."

"That happened, too," Donny said.

I thought she looked too tiny and slight for a police officer. A stiff breeze could have knocked her down, let alone an angry criminal bent on escape. A meter maid, maybe—but who knows? They have to let everybody do everything these days in spite of physical challenges, or else they'll sue you. I said, "You were a cop, huh? Where at?"

Yolanda glanced at me, then away. "Donald, I'm thirsty. Do they have water here?"

After they moved off, I escaped into the tack room. Lisa was already in there, smoke coming out of her ears. Mark joined us a moment later.

"What do you think?" I asked.

Lisa said, "You don't want to know what I think."

"She's kind of ganted up, ain't she?" Mark said.

"She's a little bitty thing, all right," I said.

Lisa said, "If I had a horse in that condition, first thing I'd do is worm her and get her teeth floated."

Then, three weeks later Donny took three days off in the middle of the week, and when he came back, he was married. He and Yolanda had zipped away to Las Vegas and exchanged vows in one of those little chapels off the strip, where the preacher was an Elvis impersonator and the wedding photos were all polaroids. Yolanda had kept most of the pictures to paste into an album one day, but Donny managed to hold onto a few, and passed them around the tack room so we could all admire them.

There they were, the happy couple, Donny wearing his good felt hat and a new checkered shirt and bolo tie, and Yolanda in a limp white dress. The dress seemed to have a fuzzy nap to it, which, along with her fuzzy hair, left her looking like pipe cleaner. The preacher towered over them, beaming proudly at the camera. He had the biggest head I'd ever seen on a man, with a massive blue-black pompadour and pointy sideburns and those big sunglasses with the shiny metal frames. Donny said this particular chapel had a drive-through lane, but they'd decided to blow the extra thirty bucks and have a stand-up wedding instead. He said it was nicer than getting married while sitting in your truck. I tried to imagine such a ceremony, with the preacher hanging out the sliding window like a clerk in a fast-food joint. When it was over he'd hand you some napkins and ask if you wanted an order of fries with that.

"You stay in a nice hotel?" Ray asked.

"The Circus Circus," Donny beamed.

"You get the bridal suite?"

"Naw, we just got a regular room. It didn't matter, we never spent hardly any time there the whole three days."

Ray looked perplexed. "You didn't spend any time in the room, on your honeymoon?"

"Yolanda likes playing slot machines. The quarter slots. She gets anxiety attacks and it helps to relax her, all those flashing lights and b-b-beepers beeping and bells ringing. She was down there in the casino most of the time."

There was a lull as we all thought about that.

"Well," Ray said. "Congratulations, Donny. I guess."

There came murmurs from around the tack room, a kind of luke-warm rumble of agreement. Then Mark said, "Where you guys gonna live?"

It was asked cautiously, as if he was scared to hear the answer. This was a detail that hadn't been discussed, and it hit all of us at the same time, that maybe Donny had her squirreled away in his room back there, and she could emerge at any moment in her nightgown, looking groggily around for a cup of coffee. Nobody wanted to see that.

Donny assured us that Yolanda was home in Escondido, and he would be commuting there on his days off, a trip of at least four hours–probably longer, given the creaky, puttery, old-man way Donny usually drove, weaving from shoulder to shoulder to centerline and back again. He'd once been given a ticket for driving too slow, the only person I'd ever heard of that happening to. To picture him braving the man-eating freeways of southern California was a startling idea. He didn't even like going to the post office on Wednesday afternoon when they had the Farmer's Market on Copenhagen Street. What would happen when those semi-trucks and Camaros and BMW sedans went streaking past him on the Ventura Freeway, people shaking their fists and cussing him and flipping him off? I could imagine him losing it completely, and stopping his truck in the emergency lane where some highway patrolman would find him, curled up on the floorboards, trembling.

Donny's days off were Thursday and Friday, every week, and had been for years and years. The following Wednesday afternoon, a wheezing, clanking little Chevy S-10 pickup pulled into the lot and parked near the gate. It had a patch of rust covering the driver's door like a skin rash. I thought at first it was somebody coming to apply for a job, this being the sort of vehicle a typical wrangler would drive. A little old man in a heavy sweater and a ball cap got out of it and hobbled toward the barn. He was bent a bit to one side, as if he'd been wadded up in there for quite a while and was stiff and sore. He saw me and waved.

"Hey! Hello, hey, you!"

"Can I help you?"

"I am here!"

"I see that," I said. "Did you need something?"

"Donald! He is ready yet?"

His accent was deeply European, but I couldn't quite place it. Some region where the women wear heavy woolen dresses and people eat a lot of sausages and garlic. He grinned at me with a mouthful of yellow teeth.

"Donald," I said. "You mean Donny?"

"Yes! I am here—you will tell him? I am the father-in-laws!"

"Donny's father in law?"

"Of course!" he said. As if it was obvious. Still grinning.

"I don't know where he is. I'll have to go find him."

"Yah, goot, goot. You go find. I wait. I will wait in the truck right here. I take a nap."

"A nap?"

"We drive back today."

In the tack room Ray was hunkered down in his folding chair, knotting a fresh lead rope onto a worn-out halter. He looked up as I came in. "Who's that guy?"

I told him. He dropped the halter and went to the door and craned his neck, as if he could see across the parking lot and into the old man's truck by pure force of will.

"Huh," he said.

I heard the feed cart pull up out back, and in a moment Donny appeared, whiskers twitching.

"Your daddy-in-law's here," Ray said.

Donny brightened. "He is?"

"He's taking a nap," I said. "He said to let you know he's waiting for you."

"He's driving me to Escondido."

"He looks kinda wore out."

"He likes to drive," Donny said.

"I hope so. That's a long trip."

Donny explained Yolanda had been worried about him making the journey south by himself, and thought it best to throw her father into the mix, an old guy who looked tired and didn't speak English very well. Then again, Donny didn't speak it all that well, either.

"He lives with Yolanda, too?" Ray asked.

"Yeah."

"How many people she got living down there?"

Donny wasn't sure. There were some kids, he said, mostly grown, who wandered in and out as the need struck them, of various ages and paternities. Dick hadn't met them all yet. And a couple of grandkids, too, he thought.

"This father-in-law," I said, "where's he from, Bulgaria or Yugoslavia or someplace like that?"

"I don't know, from over there in Europe or England or somewhere," Donny said, and then hurried off to his room to finish packing.

The rest of the crew dribbled in from various hiding places, getting ready for the two o'clock ride, and of course they were all fascinated with the idea of Donny having a father-in-law from Bulgaria or England, sleeping in his tiny pickup, and everybody wanted to creep over and get a peek at him through his window, which they immediately did, trying to look innocent and nonchalant about it—as if half a dozen people in hats and spurs should be strolling around a parking lot, surrounding a Chevy S-10 just by chance and, my goodness, look here, it's a strange little man napping behind the wheel, drooling.

It turned out that Dad wasn't asleep yet, and leaped out, delighted to meet everyone, any friend of Donny's was his friend too, and began talking in his clunky accent, talking so loudly and so quickly that most of the wranglers shrank away, losing enthusiasm, and retreated to the barn to babble to each other about the wonder of it all. Ray got pinned against the fender. The old man shouted happily at him with wide and dramatic gestures of hands and arms as he strove toward some hazy point. Ray nodded and smiled, trying to appear interested, at the same time doing his best to edge away, inch by inch. He finally broke free and hurried back to the tack room.

"I think he's from Romania," he said.

"Really?"

"I think he's a gypsy. I think they're all gypsies. They're going to suck him dry, and then you watch, they'll find him crumpled up in a ditch someplace."

And that's the way it went for the next month or so. Every Wednesday afternoon the English-Romanian-Gypsy father-in-law would roll in, wave at all of us from the parking lot, then nap until Donny finished his chores. Donny would trundle out with his duffle bag and off they'd go, down the trail to Escondido—and if that's not a Western ballad already, it should be. *Down the Trail to Escondido.*

Then, one Wednesday, the old guy didn't show. We'd gotten used to seeing him, so his absence, while not exactly worrisome, caused a twitch of curiosity. Donny never said a stuttering word about it. He went ahead with his chores that afternoon, fed the pipe pens and got his noxious coffee pot ready for the next morning same as always, and before we knew what was happening climbed into his truck and puttered off down the driveway. He didn't say goodbye, wave, honk, or explain.

Donny's truck was eight years old. For normal people that would mean it was getting some age on it, but in wrangler years it was still almost new. The age of most wrangler trucks was well into the double digits. Baling wire held many an exhaust system together, duct tape held more than a few headlights in place, and there were dents and abrasions beyond counting. The dull orange of primer was always well represented.

Not Donny's truck.

Donny had bought it new, off the lot. He took good care of it, never used it for anything as unpleasant and destructive as hauling stuff around, or pulling a trailer, or anything resembling work. He hosed the dust and fly specks off of it at least once a month, and changed the oil every time the odometer clicked past three thousand miles—which, for Donny, was about once a year. It was his pride and joy, a symbol of what he considered himself to be, because every cowboy worth his salt drove a pickup.

Two days later he rolled back to the ranch without it.

It was a little gray car, and it had a slightly crumpled back bumper that had happened a while ago because there was rust in the crumple. None of us recognized the car. It pulled around the back of the bunkhouse and parked in Donny's customary spot, and Donny climbed out of it.

He didn't look at us. Or say anything. Not a peep. He went into his room and closed the door behind him.

"Maybe that's Yolanda's little car," Lisa said. "Maybe she needed the truck to move something."

"If she needed to move something she'd make Donny move it while he was there," I said.

"I don't think he'd give her his truck, would he? I mean, true love and everything—but his truck?"

Ray said, "What kind of car is that? They all look the same these days, them little cars. You noticed that?"

We chewed it over among ourselves while saddling the horses, waiting for Donny to come out of his room and explain everything, only he never did. He called in sick that day. He actually called from his room on the phone, instead of opening his door and just hollering, which he could have. Sam took the call, listened, shook his head and hung up without comment.

Donny was back to work next morning, fussing around with his paper work same as always. I won't say he looked healthy, because Donny never really looked healthy, but he didn't look sick either. He wouldn't meet anybody's eyes. He wrote the guests' names on the big white board with his nose right up against it, and did his best to ignore everyone. He went to the lesson board and started putting up assignments there, and managed to mis-spell my name, which is a pretty good trick seeing as how it only has four letters.

Lisa said, "Did you hear? Yolanda made Donny leave his truck down south. She's going to sell it."

"Sell it? Why?"

"She wants the money, I'm guessing. She told him it's too expensive to drive. That's why she gave him the little gray car. It's cheap on gas."

"What happened to the little gypsy guy?"

She shrugged. "Who knows?"

So there it was. It had started.

The Big Drain Off.

Donny had lived on the ranch, rent free, for over thirty years. Everything he ate was out of a can. He never took a vacation—or, if he did, he just hung around the barn in his sweat pants and slippers—and he never spent money on frivolous things like soap or deodorant, so most likely he had a good chunk of cash salted away. And we were all thinking the same thing: Yolanda, with her little rat-like nose, had sniffed through the computer and smelled that money. She meant to have it. Every cent.

We spent the rest of the day not mentioning it out loud, but we'd raise our eyebrows at each other as we met going in and out of the barn. Donny paid us no attention, and went about his everyday work-avoiding maneuvers like it was the most normal thing in the world to be married to a strange woman bent on sucking the blood from his veins.

Sam said, "Donny's a little old to be learning life lessons like this."

Lisa said, "I don't think he's learned anything yet."

Donny continued to head down to Escondido—or, as Ray put it, into the lair of the Spider Woman—every week, and every week it there was some new project that required him to crack open his dusty wallet and shell out. The house needed painting. She had to have a new bedroom set. She wanted to attend a professional WWL wrestling tournament where the contestants wore colorful tights and masks, and hurled insults at each other over the microphones, and she needed signed photos of them all, and posters. Her television was broken, and she must have a new one. She wanted to go to Vegas again to play the quarter slots and relax and keep her anxiety attacks at bay. And so on.

It seemed she no longer worked at any job she might have had, whatever it was that caused her wrists to go bad and required her to wear those curious leather braces, so the only money coming in to support her and her Yugoslavian-Romanian-English father, and the slew of grown kids wandering in and out, was from her new gruff and gullible hubby.

Ranch paychecks were issued every two weeks, on Monday morning. Sam picked them up at the front office and dealt them out, white envelopes with shiny clear windows showing your name and address, and inside the pretty blue checks with the print-outs showing how many hours you worked, how many private rides and lessons you suffered through, how much was lost to taxes and what was left over at the end. We usually had them in hand before lunch. By one-thirty Yolanda was on the phone to Donny.

He actually said, "Yes, dear." We heard him do it.

"Yes, dear," he'd say. "I'll be off around three o'clock and I'll head for the bank. No, I'll go right there, f-f-first thing. I'm sorry, honey, yes, I know, but I needed some groceries last time. The cupboard was bare, you know? You know?" And he'd laugh, a dry, frantic noise, and assure her once again he would hustle along and get the check deposited so she could put her grasping little fingers on it.

We'd all cringe, and be embarrassed for him, and pretend we hadn't heard any of it, but of course we had, and once he was out of earshot would repeat it back to each other in wonderment, and shake our heads.

Then, on a blustery Wednesday just before lunch, Lisa came up to me looking serious and secretive. She had an envelope in her hand, one of those big manilla ones like they use for business papers. She said, "You got any money? Give it to me."

"What for?"

"Never mind what for."

The tone of her voice told me there was no room for negotiation. I had five dollars I'd planned to use for gas to get home. I handed it over. She stuffed it into the envelope and moved on to pin Ray against the barn wall and extort some cash out of him. Ray was notoriously tight, but Lisa was taking no guff from anyone today. She shook her finger at him and he peeled a ten and a couple of singles off his roll.

She tapped pretty much everybody. Tyrell, the chubby assistant horse shoer, tried to give her some pocket change and she hissed and growled until he thought better of it. By the time she finished, the envelope looked pretty full. Then we didn't see her for a while, until later that afternoon, when the two o'clock ride came in and we were unsaddling the horses. She approached me and said, nearly whispering, "Tomorrow after work. Five o'clock. Be here, at the picnic table outside the gate."

"What for?"

"Just be here. Don't ask questions."

So, at five o'clock Thursday afternoon, instead of sitting in a dark, stuffy bar drinking beer like sensible people, all of us were standing around the splintery picnic table next to the barn gate, wondering what the hell. Lisa sat on the bench with her arms folded, staring out at the parking lot.

"Just wait," she said. "He'll be here. Any minute."

"Who will?"

"Hush."

A few minutes later a Chevrolet Impala, at least twenty years old, hove into the lot. What little paint it had left was gray and peeling, and it listed heavily to the driver's side, like an old boat trying to make port before she capsized. It sighed to a stop and the door creaked open, and a fat man climbed laboriously out, wearing the largest pair of black business slacks I ever saw. I didn't know they made them that big, like a tent with legs. One side of his shirt tail had come untucked, and his red power tie hung loose, the way a ribbon would look stuck on a molasses barrel. He had a bad comb-over.

Ray was on the bench beside Lisa. This big man wheezed up, wiping his face with a handkerchief, and waved at him to move off. Ray scrambled out of the way just in time, and the man flopped down with a groan. The bench creaked dangerously and sank a couple inches deeper into the ground.

"Damn," the man said. "It's hot, ain't it? Are you Lisa?"

Lisa said, "This is Mr. Finch, everybody."

"Braxton Finch," the man said. "Pleezameetcha. You got the money?"

Lisa gave him the yellow envelope. Mr. Finch, still mopping his face, used his free hand to drag out the wad of bills. He looked at it like it was something he was fixing to eat, then stuffed it into his hip pocket without counting it. "That'll do, I guess," he said. "For a down payment."

"Mr. Finch is a private investigator," Lisa said.

Ray said, "A what?"

"A private detective."

"Really? Like on TV?"

"I asked him to come and help us with Donny."

"I don't usual like to take on these domestic cases," Mr. Finch said, "but things is been a little slow, and I don't guess it hurts to do folks a favor now and then."

Ray said, "I didn't know we had any private eyes around here. You got an office in town?"

"I'm a free agent," Mr. Finch said. "I don't limit myself to working out of any one place. In this business you got to be able to stick and move, bucko. Stick and move!"

"Does that mean you work out of your car?" Mark asked.

"I spend a lot of time in libraries, too. That's a good place to ferret out information, your basic library."

Ray said, "You got a gun?"

"So, what's this woman's name, this bloodsucker you want me to investigate?"

"Yolanda," Lisa said.

"Yolanda what? She got a last name?"

We all looked at each other.

"She's from Escondido," Lisa said.

"Huh. That don't help much. Yolanda from Escondido, there could be a hundred Yolandas down there. I'm a pretty good investigator, but you think we might narrow the field a bit?"

Ray said, "Her daddy's a gypsy from Europe."

"Say again?"

Lisa told him how Yolanda was draining Donny dry, and how we were all worried about him, he was ruining his life over this woman and wouldn't listen to reason, and Mr. Fitch said that was all very interesting but he still needed to know her last name. I couldn't remember ever hearing it, and apparently neither could anybody else, which left us dead in the water, pretty much. Then Ray snapped his fingers and said he remembered Donny telling him that her last name was Epperson. Yolanda Epperson.

"Jefferson?" Mr. Finch said.

"No. Epperson. I remember when he introduced us, that was her name."

Mr. Finch produced a damp little spiral notebook from his shirt pocket. "I don't suppose none of you's got a pen on him, do you?"

Of course we didn't. Lisa went over and looked in the sign-up shack, but there wasn't one there, either, nothing but dust and bird droppings.

"I got one in the car, up on the dash I think," Mr. Finch said. "I just don't feel like walking all that way."

It couldn't have been twenty feet to his car, but I guess if you tip the scales at four hundred pounds, twenty feet is a considerable distance. Ray volunteered to make the trek, opened the door to the Impala and rummaged around on the dashboard. He came back with a ballpoint that was missing its cap. It still worked, though.

"You sure got a lot of newspapers and magazines piled in that car," Ray said.

"Them's all research materials. Epperson, you say the name was?"

"Yolanda Epperson," Tim said.

"Only they just got married," Lisa said. "Her last name is Sousa now. Or maybe hyphenated, like some of those people do. Yolanda Epperson Sousa."

"Is that with a Z? Souza?"

"I don't think so."

Mr. Finch wrote that down in his little notebook and put the notebook back in his shirt pocket. "Your friend already married this person?"

"Does that mean it's too late to do anything?"

"Maybe not. What I'll be looking for is her history, her rap sheet, if you understand me. I'm looking for all the dope on her, what she's done and who she's done it to. No guarantees, you understand, but if I come up with something juicy, I'll call you. You can decide what to do with it– go to the media, or try and blackmail her out of the country, or whatever."

Ray said, "Blackmail? Really?"

"I ain't saying you should do that. That would be against the law, of course. I ain't saying you should do nothing of the kind. I'm just kinda throwing it out there."

Lisa said, "I don't think we want to go to the media."

"Whatever," Mr. Finch said. "I'm just throwing it out there. I don't suppose none of you's got a cigarette I can borrow, do you?"

None of us smoked, but Ray offered him a pinch of Copenhagen instead. Mr. Finch waved it away, then grunted to his feet and announced he'd best get to work, that the criminals and ne'er-do-wells were always up to some sort of nastiness and chicanery, but he'd flush them out, never doubt it. Whatever the hell that meant. We watched him shoe-horn himself back into his car and do a seven-point turn to get out of the parking space, and off he went, law and order's last best hope creeping down the driveway with his left turn signal blinking.

Mark said, "Where did you find him?"

Lisa said, "A friend of mine used him in her divorce. She gave me his number."

"How much did we just pay him?"

"A couple hundred dollars."

We all let out a collective gasp. This was an astronomical sum. There was no way she had managed to wheedle two hundred bucks out of a bunch of dude wranglers. It was impossible. There wasn't that much cash in the whole world, even on payday. Lisa admitted that she'd cleaned out the Wrangler Fund, too, and Ray groaned and sank back down onto the picnic bench.

"No. Say you didn't."

Lisa bristled. "Why?"

Any cash tips we might receive—and they were few and far between, but once in a while a kindly guest would take pity on us and flick a ten our way, or even a twenty—wound up in the plastic mayonnaise jar with the slot cut into the lid we called our Wrangler Fund, used for beer and barbecue and other stuff we might need, such as saddle soap, or bandages.

"That was our beer money," Mark said.

"This is about Donny. Isn't he more important than your stupid beer?"

"You could have at least asked everybody first," Ray said.

"And if I had, wouldn't you have said yes?"

"That ain't the point."

"Well? Would you?"

"I guess so. Probably."

"All right then. Shut up."

A couple weeks trickled by and we kept waiting to hear something, only we never did. Lisa called Mr. Finch at least once a day, but it went straight to voice mail every time, and he didn't seem to be in a rush to call her back.

On the following Thursday, instead of climbing into the crumpled little silver car and heading for Yolanda's place, Donny stayed in his room with the door closed, just like in the old days. You could hear his television going, game shows and soap operas. He only crept out once in the afternoon, for a trip to the post office, wearing a ball cap and squinting against the sunlight. Ray caught him, and asked what was up. Donny said Yolanda wasn't feeling well, and told him he should stay away so he wouldn't catch whatever it was she had. He thought it might be the flu, or maybe some kind of mysterious female problem, he wasn't sure. She still called him on payday, though, and pestered him about his check. She felt healthy enough to do that.

When things had dragged on long enough and still no word, Lisa said, "I'm scared Mr. Finch is playing us."

I said, "Maybe it takes a while, this detective business. He has to be sneaky, creeping around and finding stuff out. It takes time."

"You wouldn't think he'd keep our money and not do anything, would you?"

I shrugged. "Could be."

"Well," she said, "I'm not going to stand for it. We need to find him."

It was unclear how we might do that, since Finch didn't seem to have a real office anywhere and wasn't answering his phone. Then I remembered what he said about hanging out at the library, and on my way home that afternoon I swung by the combination sheriff's station-courthouse-library downtown. Sure enough, there he was, back where they keep the newspapers, reclining on the couch. He wore flip-flops and white socks along with his gigantic slacks, and didn't recognize me right away.

"Did you need to look at this copy of the *Press-Recorder*?" he asked. "I can give you the sports page if you want."

"I was figuring on talking to you."

He squinted at me. "Oh! You're one of the cowboys from that ranch, aren't you? What was that woman's name again?"

"Yolanda."

"No, the one who hired me, the skinny blond lady."

"Lisa. She's been trying to call you."

"Yes, well. I had to travel out of state for a while, tending to some sensitive business, and had to play it incognito, if you follow my meaning. But I'm back now, ready to rock and roll. You tell her that."

"Be better if you called her yourself and told her," I said. "If you follow my meaning."

"Of course, of course. I'll do that right away, soon as I have something. You know, I have a feeling about that woman, the one you wanted me to investigate, Jefferson or Hepperson or whatever her name is—"

"Yolanda."

"Yeah, whatever, that one. You get a feel for these things when you been at it long as I have. You sense stuff. And this Yolanda woman, lurking down there in Encino, she's got something going on, something sneaky. I can smell it."

"Escondido."

"Say again?"

"She's lurking in Escondido, not Encino."

"Oh, right, right. Well, she's got something going on, wherever she lives, take my word for it. I have a definite feel for these things."

Donny started acting strange the next couple of days, and I mean strange even for Donny. He was tense and nervous, all his movements became kind of sudden and jerky, and if you asked him a question he'd snap at you and scuttle away and pretend like you were talking to somebody else. And cranky? Man, oh man, he was like an old mare, his ears constantly pinned back. We all perked up at this development, and were hopeful, thinking it might mean there was trouble in paradise and the problem was taking care of itself. Then we discovered that Yolanda had just made him quit dipping Copenhagen.

It was Ray figured it out. Ray was over fifty years old, but still acted like everybody's evil little brother, and if he could find a way to needle you, he'd do it. Donny was at the big wooden desk in the tack room, whipping up a stiff breeze as he sorted the week's liability waivers into something that vaguely resembled alphabetical order. Ray took out a brand-new tin of Copenhagen, ran the tip of his knife blade around the edge of the lid and popped it open. He waved it under Donny's nose.

"Want a dip of snoose, Donny?"

Donny flapped a hand at him. "Get away from me, Ray."

"You sure? It's real fresh."

"Get away from me!"

Ray looked at the rest of us and grinned. "Donny's quit chewing. Ain't that right, Donny?"

"Just never mind!"

"Really?" Lisa said.

This was unthinkable. Donny had dipped Copenhagen since he was three years old, give or take a few years. The bulge of snuff in his bottom lip was just a part of him, the same as his eyeglasses, or the hair in his ears. It had been the source of many a complaint from ranch guests who were completely grossed out by it, as Donny tended to dribble, both down his chin and onto his shirt. But, still—there are a few things in a man's life that should remain sacred, and a good dip of Copenhagen first thing in the morning with your coffee was right up there at the top of the list.

Donny said, "Yolanda says it costs too much money, and it's disgusting. A disgusting habit, she says."

Mark said, "So?"

"So, she made me quit."

Ray waved the tin. "C'mon, Donny. Take a big ol' whiff!"

Donny let out a squawk and stood up, nearly knocking over his chair. He stormed out, and we heard him stomp all the way to his room, and the door slam.

Lisa said, "That's mean."

"Yes, it is," Ray cackled.

"How did you know he'd quit? Did he tell you?"

"I recognized the signs. I quit myself, once. Worst twenty minutes of my life."

Lisa shook her head. "Wow. First his pickup, now his tobacco. She's taking away his manhood."

This went on for about a day and a half, and to be honest was kind of fun to watch. We were all decent people, wanting to do right and support our friend, so of course the first thing we did was make bets with each other as to how quick Donny would fall off the wagon—and no fair waving tobacco under his snoot like Ray had done. This had to happen naturally. The pool got all the way up to twelve bucks.

He chewed about forty sticks of gum that first morning, but he wasn't very good at it, and wound up biting his own tongue five or six times. You could hear him all the way across the corral every time it happened— "Ouch! Damn it!"—and just before lunch he gave up and threw the gum into the trash can. He found a bag of peppermint candies in his room and went to sucking on them instead, leaving a trail of wrappers behind him on the ground like he was trying to find his way out of the enchanted forest.

He couldn't sit still, either—never could, really, but now he was even more nervous. He'd bounce off the walls in the tack room for a while, then drive the feed cart out to the pipe pens and back, and make a couple of trips to the front office for no good reason, where he spoke to the girls at the desk in a frantic way, talking very, very fast about nothing in particular. He sweated a good deal, too. We all watched with predatory interest, keeping an eye on the clock and thinking about that twelve dollars and what we could do with it.

Sam said, "As a boss, it wouldn't be right if I ordered him to go back to his bad habits, would it?"

Lisa said, "They say nicotine is one of the hardest addictions to kick. It's like trying to get off heroin."

"He's driving me nuts. I'm not trying to kick any addiction, why should I have to suffer? If he flits through here one more time I'm going to scream."

"His eyes look sort of haunted, don't they?"

My bet was he'd lose it by three o'clock, but Donny hung in there, I had to hand it to him. He was, in fact, still clean and upright at the end of the day, which surprised all of us. Lisa offered the hopeful opinion that the first day or two were the worst, but Ray said he didn't think so. He thought they were all bad, and would continue to be bad right up to the point where you threw yourself off a bridge.

Donny was so discombobulated that he forgot to make his nasty coffee, so next morning we had to sneak over to the employee dining room and get some there, which was an improvement and made everybody feel better, except for Donny. He was deep into his battle with the evil tobacco monster, and was really sweating now. His knuckles were white. We watched him go through his daily chores in a lifeless, mechanical way, like somebody had whacked him over the head with a brick, and stunned him. He wouldn't talk, or look at you if you said something to him—even

Ray, who tried constantly to get a rise out of him, until Sam made him stop it.

We sensed a breakdown was coming, but he'd already out-lasted every prediction so we had to place our bets for the twelve dollars all over again. Even the girls who cleaned the guest cottages were talking about it, mostly in Spanish, and laying down their own bets, and so were the grounds maintenance guys and even the people way over at the golf course, though how they managed to hear about it was beyond me, or why they'd care. Nosy bystanders. The whole ranch was a-twitter.

Then Lisa said, "Mr. Finch wants to meet with us at Giovanni's. He thinks he's got something."

This time only me and Lisa and Ray decided to go. Everyone else had more important stuff to do, like watching television or sorting their sock drawers. Giovanni's was a loud place with sawdust on the floor and red-checkered tablecloths, and video games in the back. They sold beer by the pitcher and gave you a real glass to drink it with, and any kind of pizza you wanted, as long as it was pepperoni. Mr. Finch was gasping at a table near the rest rooms when we got there about five-thirty, but he hadn't ordered anything yet. He said he was waiting on us.

"If I'm gonna keep this up I'll need some more money from you people," he said.

"There ain't no more money," Lisa said.

"I got some expenses, you know. The cost of doing business and all that."

I said, "I didn't think they charged you for sitting around the library."

Lisa said, "Not a farthing more."

Mr. Finch sighed, and dabbed at his face with his handkerchief. It looked like the same one from the other day. "Yeah, well, I figgered as much. We'll mark that invoice paid in full, shall we? Another small businessman circling the drain. But only because you're trying to help your friend, and I'm a big softy. It's my downfall, being so kind and tender-hearted all the time. Ask anybody. And if I was you, I'd tell your friend to watch his hind end, because this Yolanda woman has already shot one husband."

There was a hollow sound as our jaws hit the table. Lisa said, "Excuse me?"

Ray said, "You're kidding."

Mr. Finch grinned. "You know, it's pretty reasonable, what they charge for a pitcher of beer in this establishment."

We scraped together what money we had and ordered a pitcher of Coors Light, and then he wanted a pizza, too, pepperoni and mushrooms if that was possible. Lisa put it on her credit card. We watched as Mr. Finch inhaled four slices of pizza and three glasses of beer in about a minute and a half.

"The thing is," he said, still chewing, "this Yolanda woman's had three husbands already, but I can't find a record of any divorces. You know what that means."

"She's still married?" Ray suggested.

"It means she's a bigamist! That's illegal in *my* United States of America, I don't know about yours."

"Then her marriage to Donny isn't legal, either," Lisa said, brightening like a little ray of sunshine.

Mr. Finch pointed a stubby finger. "Bingo."

Ray said, "Skip ahead to where she shoots the guy. I wanna hear that part."

Mr. Finch said he had a friend who was a retired detective from San Diego, and he's the one told him about it. Said he remembered Yolanda right away, soon as he heard the name, on account of she used to work for the police department down there.

"So she really was a cop?" I said.

"Nah, she weren't no officer. She worked in some cubicle doing clerical stuff, but this detective remembered her on account of she shot somebody. A thing like that makes a person stand out in your memory."

He said that one of Yolanda's previous husbands, number two or number three—he wasn't sure which one, exactly—had been a no-good abusive son of a buck, and every time he got a few cocktails in him he'd want to slap Yolanda around. The neighbors called the police on several occasions when they heard him hollering and Yolanda screaming, and the cops came and talked to them and made notes, but Yolanda would never press charges so what could they do?

"Finally, one night I guess she had all she could take, and when he got to thumping on her she grabbed a gun and shot him. Got him right in the leg."

"She didn't kill him?" Lisa said.

"No, but they say he bled all over the dining room carpet. It was a white carpet, and you know that ain't ever coming out."

"What happened to her?" Ray asked. "They put her in jail for it?"

"Not even close. The judge who heard the case was an old hard-nose, no wishy-wash or bleeding hearts allowed in his courtroom, by God. He decreed from the bench that the wounded husband was nothing but a festering pimple on the backside of the body politic and got exactly what he had coming to him. Said Yolanda deserved a medal for doing society a favor and putting him out of action. Dismissed all charges and told her to go forth and sin no more. Anybody else going to eat that last slice of pizza?"

"Maybe we could ease him into it," I said. "Give him a little information at a time, bit by bit. Let him get used to it."

No, Lisa wanted to take all the news to Donny right away and lay it out for him, boom, as subtle as a brick through a window. Rip that band-aid off, no pussy-footing or dilly-dallying. She was certain the bigamy thing would tip the balance, since it nulled and voided the matrimonial bonds—though the idea of Yolanda picking off husbands with a handgun like paper ducks on the midway was also troubling.

"Take away her meal ticket and she might get mad," Ray said. "Shoot one husband, it makes shooting the next one all that easier."

"She won't shoot anybody," Lisa said.

"Famous last words."

In the end we agreed to sleep on it, and figure what to do tomorrow. Ray wanted to stay and drink more beer, but we'd run out of money and Mr. Finch wasn't about to buy anything.

The next morning a trailer load of new horses rolled in from the broker in Wyoming. We'd been expecting them for a week, but horse brokers can be vague when it comes to exact delivery dates. Ray and Mark and I got them situated in the quarantine pens on the south side of the arena. We set up the water troughs and threw them some hay and spent a while looking them over. They were generic dude horses, sorrels and bays, big-footed and a little drawn up from standing in a stock trailer for two days. Ray told them, "Welcome to hell, boys."

When we got back to the barn we discovered the ancient green percolator was once again full of what passed for coffee around here, and Donny had caved in to addiction, his lower lip once again full of inky black snuff and his chin and shirt front full of dribbles. A degree of normalcy had returned. And Lisa was full of purpose.

"Let's get this over with," she said.

"You sure?" I said.

Ray said, "I got to run home for a minute. I think I forgot something."

"You aren't going anywhere. Come on."

So much for talking it over. The flash of her eyes and the set of her jaw told us there was no room for argument. She snatched Donny by the earlobe and dragged him to the shoeing slab and we all stood there, uncomfortable as hell, while she lowered the boom. Told him every little bit of it.

Donny blinked at us.

"I already knew that," he said.

That brought the proceedings to a screeching halt. Ray actually laughed.

Lisa looked stunned. "Really?"

"Yolanda told me about it a long time ago."

"What about that part where she never got divorced yet?"

Donny shrugged. "That's probably just the paperwork got lost. It don't matter."

This was where I expected Lisa to wag her finger at him, and lecture him about how the marriage wasn't official and here was the perfect chance to get free if he wanted, but one look at her told me that she'd lost all heart.

Then Donny said, "I never thought anybody would want me. Now somebody does." He shrugged again, and wandered off to find his clipboard.

Every once in a while, you get your hat handed to you. This was one of those times. We stood there and stared at each other like a bunch of idiots, and then it was over and we each remembered other stuff we needed to be doing right then.

Things sort of settled down after that. Summer was coming, and the ranch was getting busier, so we had less time to meddle in things we shouldn't be meddling in. I saw Mr. Finch in the grocery store a couple of weeks later, but he didn't recognize me. He asked me where they kept the yogurt in this place. I told him I didn't know.

Yolanda still calls Donny and pesters him about his check, but less often than she used to. Donny still makes the trip down to Escondido, but not every week. Sometimes it's just once a month. I don't know if that's because he's run completely out of money, or the honeymoon's over, or just what. All I know is it ain't none of my business.

COPENHAGEN SNUFF AND THE RESILIENCE OF STUPIDITY

I T WAS A kid named Andy Anderson who showed up with the stuff, no doubt pilfered from his father, who was known to chew it constantly, a big wad stuffed in his jaw from early morning until bedtime. Andy's father was a cowboy for the Huasna Land & Cattle Company, a princely status we all aspired to. Legend had it every time he went to town he bought a whole carton, so he'd never run out, an idea that was simply amazing to me. I seldom had more than fifty cents in my pocket at one time, so I couldn't imagine buying a carton of anything. But everybody said it, so it had to be true.

Cotton Thomas, one of my best friends, a big-boned ranch kid with a reddish crew cut, stomped up to me at lunchtime recess. "Come on," he said.

"Come on where?"

"Out to the back fence. Andy's got him a pouch of Beechnut."

Holy cow. Contraband, and the most serious kind. Mere possession was considered an actual crime, and if they caught you with it, or even near it, they expelled you, and your old man beat the hell out of you when you got home. Dangerous stuff. So, of course, we immediately headed for the dusty, weed-infested baseball diamond at the far edge of the school-yard.

If you are looking for the old tale of the dumb kids who try chewing tobacco for the first time and then get violently sick—and ain't that a funny story, har-dee-har-har—you won't find it here. Nobody got sick, or even mildly nauseous, or dizzy. At least not this time.

When you are a thirteen-year-old boy, eaten up with anxiety and the frantic misery of adolescence, the milestones of life start barreling toward you with amazing speed. Among these, and some of the most important, are the first time you get to drive the pickup, the first time you actually consider the possibility of kissing a girl, and the first time you try chewing tobacco. I'd been driving the family pickup—around the ranch mostly, not actually on the highway—since I was ten, so that was no big deal. And the girl thing was completely out of the question. If a female, any female except my mother, so much as looked at me I lost the ability to speak, or think, or even function as a human bean, and would blush so furiously red that smoke steamed up from my collar. So, chewing tobacco, and learning to do it with authority, was the only achievable goal left to me.

Andy, a skinny kid with a shock of brownish hair that stuck up all over the place, sported the same frayed denim jacket he always had on, worn nearly white at the elbows and broken threads hanging like fringe from the bottom of it. He waited at the splintery backstop with Vince Palmer, which was weird. Vince was a town kid who'd never shown any interest in cowboys or horses or any of the stuff we liked. He preferred wearing tennis shoes, and playing basketball. What he was doing out here was a mystery.

"Hey, dudes," Andy said. He grinned at us, showing the gap where his missing incisor used to be. It got knocked out a couple of weeks earlier when Cotton threw a rock at him for some unknown reason and accidentally connected. Andy said, "You want some of this?"

He hiked up his pantleg, exposing one bony shin, and reached into the boot top to pluck out a shiny red and white pouch. It was brand new, so full that the sides bulged, the colors so bright they took your breath away. He pulled it open, and there was the silvery foil of the insides. It was the legendary foil-fresh pouch you saw in all the advertisements.

Wow. This was the real deal. Real grown-up stuff, a threshold we were about to step across, though I knew both Cotton and Andy had chewed before. But not me, and for sure Vince hadn't, either.

"So, what do you do?" Vince asked, his voice a bit wavery, and I was mighty glad he did because I wasn't so sure myself. I was happy to let him be the one to sound like a doofus, instead of me.

Andy used three fingers to pluck up a wad of tobacco. "You just get you a little of it, and lay it in your cheek, like this." He demonstrated. "Then just let her sit there. Don't swaller none of the juice. Spit when you need to."

Cotton reached in with his big clunky fingers and crammed an impressive plug into his mouth. He worked it around a bit with his tongue to get everything settled, an expression of luxurious pleasure on his homely face, then spat a brown stream onto the grass. "Man, that's good."

Vince, looking worried, used the tips of two fingers to pinch out a tiny, tiny morsal, less than it would take to fill a hollow tooth, and tucked it into the proper spot. After ten seconds his face got very red, and he began to spit—but he hung in there, and did not unload the tobacco.

It was my turn. I reached into the cavernous depths of the foil-fresh pouch and got me some, not too much but not too little, either, because too little would make a guy look like a weenie. The stuff was black and curly and glistening. I crammed it into my cheek and grinned at everybody to show how happy I was, though it was not going to be a delicious experience, I could tell that right off. I immediately began to sweat under my hair.

Cotton said, "How come you want to try this, Vince? You ain't no cowboy."

Vince seemed preoccupied. He spat again, and mumbled something about baseball players and how they liked to chew at the ball field, and we all agreed this was true, having seen it on television: baseball players scratching themselves and tugging at their clothes and spitting decisively, their cheeks pooched with tobacco.

Andy said, "You guys keep a sharp eye for the teacher on yard duty, right? Don't want nobody wandering over here."

Cotton, speaking with the easy confidence of the true professional, began a lengthy dissertation upon the different brands of chew, their advantages and disadvantages. "You ever try Day's Work? Man, that'll torch a hole through you."

Andy said, "I think Skoal's the best. It's got that wintergreen flavor."

I agreed, even though I'd never heard of it until that very moment. Every ounce of moisture in my body was boiling into my mouth, a freshet of saliva that was like an emergency, and the need to spit was constant. The flavor was thick, sickly sweet and rich. A trickle leaked down the back of my throat and burned like acid. I spat, and spat again. My spit wasn't as brown as everybody else's, and I wondered if maybe I wasn't doing it right.

Cotton went on, "Me and my Dad was out cutting wood last fall, and he had him a pouch of Red Man, and he give me some. Man, I really like that stuff. It's a lot smoother than this Beechnut, I think. We chewed it all day long, working with them chainsaws. Big old Husqvarna chainsaws, twenty-four inchers. He let me drink a beer with him, too."

Pretty quick Vince said, "I got to go. There's an extra credit project I have to finish in Mr. Heine's room. See you guys later." He whirled on his sneakers and trotted off. After a few steps we saw him spit out his plug.

Andy said, "He's gonna run right to the water fountain and wash out his mouth. You watch."

We all chuckled, feeling much superior, for we were indeed manly-type men, who could chew tobacco and swagger and brag, and slap each other on the backs and congratulate ourselves on being more mature and wiser than any of the other kids at Orchard Junior High. But, naturally, as soon as the bell rang a few minutes later, we all spit the stuff out and headed for the drinking fountain, too.

I could say that this was the beginning of it, my rocky, decades-long relationship with the demon weed. But that wouldn't be accurate. At that point in my life I had already been intimate with it for thirteen years. The house I lived in was full of tobacco smoke. I breathed it in all day, every day. There were ashtrays all over the place, in every room, even the bathrooms, overflowing with bent and mashed cigarette carcasses, smelling of ash and stale nicotine, reminders that tobacco was an intrinsic part of life, a bosom friend, a companion, as indispensable to everyday existence as food, or coffee, or television.

My father smoked incessantly, three or four packs a day, using the stub end of one cigarette to light the next, sucking on them with a grim intensity, pulling the smoke deep into his lungs and blowing it out again through his mouth and nostrils in a way that made you think of dragons in caves. My brothers and I had spent endless hours cooped up in a car or the cab of a truck, going down the road with him while he filled it with smoke, a sealed atmospheric chamber, none of us ever feeling the need to roll down a window or crack a wind-wing. This is, no doubt, why chewing tobacco didn't make me sick. Nicotine didn't bother me. I'd been soaking in it for years. Every cell in my body was dripping with it.

I was in no way unique. All the kids I knew were in the same boat.

Tobacco was everyone's friend in those days. If your parents didn't smoke, you were considered odd, and perhaps a little untrustworthy. In every restaurant, movie theater, hardware store or food mart, cigarette smoke swirled up around the ceiling, cigarette butts were scattered like confetti. Tobacco was a fashion accessory, as ubiquitous as a purse, or underwear, or a necktie. To leave the house without it was unthinkable, and could actually cause panic. I saw it happen myself, several times, the old man in great distress patting at his shirt pocket only to realize he'd left his Viceroys at home. He'd usually end up growling at my mother for allowing such a horrible thing to happen, then speed to the nearest liquor store to resupply. You had to have a fancy lighter, too, a Zippo with a Marine Corps insignia on it. It would make a distinct *ping* when you deftly flicked it open and scratched it alight. It was an important sound, that *ping*, as recognizable as the old man's hacking cough in the morning, or the honk when he blew his nose.

Everything we saw reinforced the habit:

Walt Garrison, a sports hero, an athlete, showed us how to place a pinch of smokeless tobacco between our cheeks and gums.

Pretty people, with perfect hair and spotless clothes, frolicked across green and grassy fields, ecstatic over the orgasmic experience of Salem cigarettes.

Cowboys galloped their horses across sagebrush flats, chasing wild cattle and letting us know they'd be nowhere near as masculine without their Marlboros.

And, of course, James Bond, lighting his Moreland cigarette while ordering a martini that was shaken and not stirred. Impeccable in his tuxedo, and you knew there was a Walther PPK under that jacket somewhere. Cool. Dangerous.

Holy shit, weren't you supposed to use tobacco? Didn't everybody? Wasn't it like a law? Was abstaining nothing more than a character flaw?

For an awkward kid, plagued with pimples, who gets yelled at all the time, and feels the need to create some sort of identity for himself that goes beyond just being a dork, tobacco is an easy stage prop to latch onto. Especially if you've already decided that rodeo and cowboy hats and horses and cows are going to be part of that identity. Every contestant we ever saw pictured in *Rodeo Sports News* had a tin of Skoal or Copenhagen on him, usually trying to wear out the back pocket of his Wranglers. It was part of the uniform: Resistol hat, Tony Lama boots, belt buckle (a shiny silver one, please), and snoose can. We all had to have one, too, or risk being excluded from the club.

My old man was not on board with this, by the way. Not at all. Nicotine fiend though he was, the perfect example of a bad example, no son of his was going down that road, not if he could help it. My behavior was closely watched, constantly criticized, the subject of warning growls and outright threats.

"You better not let me catch you with that crap in your mouth," he said. "I'll kick your ass clean up between your shoulder blades."

He was not a fan of rodeo in the first place. He mistrusted it, because it wasn't football. He'd been a football star himself in high school, and felt it was only natural and proper that all his offspring play football, too, and make him proud. Instead, we all wanted to rodeo, and be cowboys. My old man had a curled lip and sour attitude when it came to cowboys, particularly rodeo cowboys, because they were notoriously shiftless, and never had any money, and drank a lot of beer—Coors, mostly, in those days—and climbed into their pickups after and roared around and got into trouble. Chewing tobacco was just another small step down that path to hell, and he wasn't standing for it.

So, it was bizarre that he ended up on the board of the Young Farmer's Junior Rodeo, held the first Saturday after the Fourth of July every year at the local fairgrounds.

One of his partners in the feedlot business was a mover and shaker in the local Young Farmers chapter, an advocacy group for agricultural folk, and he was the one who talked him into it. The old man griped and complained about having to do it, but he was trapped. They put him in charge of some measly category, overseeing the food vendors or something like that, which meant he had to be present for the whole thing, from dawn to dusk, an event he resented for helping to lead his children astray.

Steer riding was my event, and I sucked at it. Let me make that clear. I wanted to be good at it, I dreamed and fretted and prayed about being good at it, I imagined myself strutting around town with that silver trophy buckle, the envy of my friends who were all failures; but I was like the tubby, short guy who wants to play forward for the L.A. Lakers—desire alone was not enough to defeat reality. Had I ever won anything, even a ribbon, the old man might have conjured up the tiniest whiff of enthusiasm, but in those days they were not handing out awards for participation, and I, alas, was anything but an athlete. My coordination, shaky at the best of times, vanished like a fart in a tornado when you lashed me onto the back of a steer.

Behind the chutes at any junior rodeo, you'd see a hundred kids in brand new hats, milling about with their leather gloves and bull ropes, cow bells clanking, waiting their turn at a chance for death and dismemberment, watching as the crew prodded a seemingly endless line of steers through the bucking chutes. Contestants' names were called, chute gates opened and we all witnessed another unfortunate get pitched off onto his head in the dirt. Mostly, the victim would leap up and scamper to the fence, occasionally one of them would end up crying, usually a little kid, and every so often there'd be some blood, or even a broken arm. About once every fifty tries someone made the entire eight seconds to the buzzer, and people cheered and applauded. This, as I say, did not happen often enough to become tedious. There was plenty of time to worry about what was in store for you, if your wreck would become part of junior rodeo lore, and if they'd put up a plaque somewhere to commemorate you after you were dead. By the time my name got called I had generally cobbled up six or seven scenarios in my head involving ambulances and morticians, and every muscle in my body was tight as a new bob wire fence.

"Jesus, kid, loosen up a little," the chute boss would say, as they cinched my hand into the bull rope.

It was useless advice. I was too tense, too stiff, pitched too far forward over the steer's back, and the gate would swing wide, I'd make three, maybe four jumps, then the ground would hit me in the face. This happened, the same way, the same mouthful of dirt, four or five times a year, or however many rodeos I entered. Jim Shoulders and Larry Mahan had nothing to fear from me.

It was early afternoon. Lunch break was over and the girl's barrel racing had just finished. The steer riding event was underway. Cotton Thomas and I were behind the chutes, gloves full of rosin and hearts full of fear. The tinny speaker hanging from the announcer's stand crackled off something I didn't quite catch.

Cotton said, "You hear that?"

"What?"

"Bobby Nunes just got pitched off."

"Wow. What about Billy Nunes?"

The Nunes brothers were a couple of years older. They were hotshots, deadly at roping as well as rough stock, arrogant competitors who looked down upon the rest of us insects with disdain.

"I don't think he's been up yet. You want a chew?"

"Hell yes," I said.

We were occupied at what was known, in accepted rodeo vernacular, as heating up our riggings. You hung your bull rope from the pipe fence, poured a small pile of rosin from your Bull Durham pouch onto your leather glove, then worked it into the hand loop of the bull rope, grinding it deep into the hemp. The friction was supposed to make everything sticky, creating a more secure grip. There were forty kids around us, all busy at the same task. It was more ceremonial than practical, as your glove was usually in the hand loop only a couple of seconds before you became airborne.

I was already tensing up, same as always, my nerves twanging like banjo strings.

Cotton produced the tin of Copenhagen that we'd procured early that morning at a liquor store a couple blocks from the fairgrounds. He thumbed open the lid and offered it to me with a flourish. I took a gigantic three-fingered dip and pressed it into my lip, as was the proper form. Cotton did likewise.

It had to be a huge dip, so ponderous that your lower lip pooched way out and the black snuff was visible. Visibility, that was the important thing. This was not about tobacco enjoyment. This was performance art. People had to see that you had it, so they could be impressed, and envy you.

"When are we up?" Cotton asked.

I stepped over and consulted the mimeographed list, taped to the flaking green paint of a nearby fence post. "There's ten or twelve ahead of us," I said. "Then I go, and you're right after me."

"We'll be in the chutes at the same time."

"Yep."

"Partners!"

"Yep," I said, and spat a healthy stream, and didn't get hardly any on me. My spit was now nice and dark. I had learned, over many months, how to do it properly.

That's when the old man walked around the corner in his taco-shaped cowboy hat.

He wasn't supposed to be back here. He never came behind the chutes. Ever. If he wasn't fussing over some administrative detail with the food vendor people, he was plopped in the grandstands next to my mother, smoking cigarettes and looking sullen. But here he was, thundering toward us like a storm, scowling as usual, and me with my lip stuffed full of enough Copenhagen to choke a horse. My ass was about to be kicked clean up between my shoulder blades.

I didn't even think. I had only one move open to me, and I took it. My tongue performed a deft sweep across my bottom teeth, swept the wad of snuff to the back of my mouth, and I swallowed it.

"How you boys doing?" the old man asked.

"Okay," I squeaked.

"We're fine," Cotton said, grinning. "How are you, sir?" I saw, horrified, that Cotton's teeth were flecked with tobacco. It looked as though he'd been licking the pepper shaker. I hoped the old man wouldn't notice.

"All set? Ready to go?"

"Yessir," I said.

"You bet!" Cotton said.

"How soon you up?"

"Pretty quick," I said, feeling very puzzled. Why the sudden interest? What the hell was he doing here, what could he possibly want?

"You know there ain't nobody got one rode yet," the old man said. "The field's wide open."

"Yessir."

"You boys seen Tom Pryor back here anywhere?"

"I seen Mr. Pryor go up to the announcer's booth a few minutes ago," Cotton said.

"Oh. Okay, good. I'll find him," the old man said, then actually gave us a smirk, about the closest thing to a smile as he ever mustered. "Well. Good luck."

"Thanks!" Cotton said. All I could manage was a weak nod. The old man clapped me on the back—another thing he never, ever did—and strode away.

Cotton said, "That was nice of him, wishing us luck."

"I guess so."

I did a quick inventory. The back of my throat had a nasty taste to it, and sizzled with bright heat. My sinuses began to fill, and my eyes watered. My stomach was okay, so far, but I feared what the next few minutes might bring. I had eaten a bowl of chili and a hot dog for lunch. I turned back to my bull rope. It was like I'd never seen it before, and I realized I was no longer interested in heating up my rigging. I could feel my heart thudding inside my ears.

"Man," I said, "what in *hell* was he doing here?"

"Looking for Mr. Pryor. You heard him. What's wrong?"

"I swallowed my chew."

His eyes got very wide. "You what?"

"What was I supposed to do? If I'd spit it out he'd of seen me, wouldn't he?"

"Man, oh, man. You going to be sick?"

"No. I don't know. I'm all right. So far."

I unlooped my bull rope from the rail and slung it over my shoulder. Cotton was staring at me, an intense, expectant stare that had some real terror in it, as if he were scared I might explode any second.

We heard Billy Nunes' name announced over the tin speaker, and shoved our way to the arena fence to watch. Billy was the guy who always took first in this event, the guy to beat, only nobody ever did, unless it was his brother. It was rumored that their dad, who was really mean, made them get on two or three steers every night before he'd even let them eat supper. They had a whole pen of nasty, huge Corriente cattle they practiced on. Between Billy and his brother, they owned more silver buckles than the display case at Wilson's Western Wear, downtown.

The chute gate swung wide, and out he came. Sitting back, exactly the way you were supposed to, right arm held high and away, butt flat against the steer's hide and never a glimpse of daylight showing, the steer jumping and bawling, twisting. Billy spurred him like a saddle bronc rider. It was beautiful and impressive. Intimidating.

All of us were shouting. The people in the stands woke from their torpor and actually clapped a little. It looked like Billy had him rode, he was going to make the buzzer, another winning ride for the Nunes family. The steer took one last twist to the east, bawled, the ducked sharply to the west—

And Billy fell off. On his head. With his legs in the air.

"*Ooooooh!*"

The moan went up from every mouth present, contestants and audience alike, everybody realizing, in the same instant, that they'd just witnessed something historical.

The buzzer buzzed.

The Nunes' had goose-egged.

Cotton was shouting, right into my face. I couldn't make out what he was saying, exactly, something about how anybody could win it now. Something. Whatever. The first wave of dizziness hit me, a sudden, woozy feeling. The world swayed, like I'd stepped onto a boat. I grabbed the fence.

"Whoa."

Cotton grabbed my shirt. "You okay?"

"Whoa," I said.

"You gonna puke? Hey, don't get it on me, okay?"

Someone was saying my name, over and over again. From far away, way off in the distance. I shook my head, trying to clear it. The boat was really rocking now.

"You're up!" Cotton shouted.

"I don't—"

"They're calling you! Go! You have to go now!"

He pushed me, and I almost went down. My legs had turned to butter, but he kept pushing, and got me to the wooden catwalk where the chute boss, a fat man with a clipboard, was still hollering my name.

"I was about to turn your steer out, Mister."

"Whoa."

Somebody grabbed my bull rope. I found myself standing over the broad, fly-specked back of a gigantic horned beast, the biggest steer I'd ever seen, almost an ox, and the beast was angry, roiling, fighting, trying to crawl up and over the rails as the crew struggled to get my rigging around him.

Can't get sick, can't get sick, can't get—

"Come on, kid!"

My stomach was churning now, sloshing and bubbling, a cauldron on the boil, and under there somewhere a ball of hot lead was trying to rise into the back of my throat.

"Climb on, boy," the chute boss griped. "I ain't gonna put a saddle on him for you."

It was as if someone else was settling down onto that steer, someone else fitting his hand into the loop and feeling it draw tight. When you ask for the gate you're supposed to say, "Outside!" or "Pull the trigger!" or something tough and macho-Western like that. It's an important part of the tradition, a thing you look forward to, shouting those words. I didn't even care. I just nodded. I think I nodded—I may have only tilted to one side and they took it for a nod. The gate swung open and we plunged into the arena.

It felt like I was watching it from someplace else. The wild revolt going on inside my body had disconnected me completely from steers and rosined gloves and jabbering contestants and the rest of it, and for the first time in my life I wasn't tensed up—no, I was limp as a shoestring, flopping and flapping, my head waggling loosely at the end of my neck. The steer jumped one way and I went with him. I didn't care. He jumped the opposite way and I bounced right along, my mind as fuzzy as a bag of cotton balls. He bawled and snorted. I wasn't impressed. He twisted and jerked and lunged, all very interesting but it was happening to someone else, and I heard applause coming from somewhere, and a buzzer go off, but I just kept rocking along.

"Get off him, kid! The bell rang!"

It was one of the clowns, running alongside.

"Jump off! You got him rode!"

Oh. Okay.

I piled off. I just let go. The steer's momentum wafted me gently into the air, where I performed a graceful pirouette and landed, amazingly, on my feet. The crowd in the stands, all two dozen of them, cheered.

From the corner of my eye I saw another gate swing out, and here came Cotton. His steer took two jumps and went into a spin. Cotton stayed with him, sitting upright and just a little back, the right way, and he was spurring, spurring hard, perfect form, perfect ride. I didn't hang around to watch the rest of it. I crawled over the arena fence, found a convenient bush beside the sorting alley, and was quietly sick.

We wound up taking first and second. Cotton got the silver buckle and I received the red ribbon, an anemic little award but the first time I'd ever won anything, in any competition. We met behind the chutes and congratulated each other. The Two Musketeers. Butch and Sundance. Frick and Frack. I was shaky and weak, and my head was pounding. Cotton kept saying, "Did you see that? Did you *see* that?" over and over. All I could do was smile, but it was a tepid smile, with not a lot of energy behind it.

You might think I'd been taught a lesson that day. Any reasonable person would think that, but of course you'd be wrong. I considered it merely a bump in the road, nothing to worry about, nothing to learn, and continued on my merry way. It's amazing how resilient stupidity can be.

Later that afternoon, sitting at a picnic table next to the hot dog stand, Cotton whipped out the Copenhagen and pushed it toward me.

"Want a chew?"

I looked at it. Things had begun to settle down. My head didn't hurt anymore. "Maybe," I said. "But just a little one."

SNARKY T.V.

WE DON'T HAVE television at our house. It was a decision we made several years ago after realizing we could click our way through a hundred channels and find nothing worth watching, and we were paying a good chunk of money every month for the privilege. It seemed a silly thing to be doing, so we pulled the plug.

Getting weaned was tough, especially for me, because, being a guy, I am genetically predisposed to sitting on the couch eating potato chips and staring at a screen where inane things are going on. It's in every man's DNA, right there next to the part that makes you want to scratch yourself in public or leaf through the Sports Illustrated Swimsuit Edition at the news stand when you think nobody's looking. But I struggled through, and got some distance on it, and can proudly say I'm completely cured of the habit. Until, when out on the road, I check into a motel room somewhere. The first thing I do is flick the dreaded thing on. I grab the remote and scroll through forty or fifty or a hundred and twenty channels, whatever's available in the town I find myself in, and discover—surprise!—there's still nothing on.

It's all the same show. Every production is about a group of people between the ages of 23 and 33, living in a stylish urban setting, all of them very slim and fit with good teeth, teeth that are white and straight like chiclets, saying snarky things to each other. This seems to be the whole point. Everybody walks around with a curled lip, looking very fashionable and sexy, being caustic and snide, and at the end of the episode whoever the star of the show is gets off the snarkiest bit of dialog and the show is over until next week—or until the next program comes on and the same thing starts all over again with a different cast, all of which are interchangeable. Even if it's a cop show, solving the crime is of secondary concern. The real purpose of the mystery is to allow the clever and biting repartee to occur between the characters.

The only variance in an evening's line-up is the so-called reality show full of rednecks with scraggly beards and exaggerated southern accents. These rednecks are also interchangeable. They dig for gold or make moonshine or wrestle with alligators, and they all seem to be the same bunch of morons. I can almost hear the directors shouting at them between shots. *"You're not acting stupid enough!"* Because everybody knows if you don't live in town you are a hick, and hicks are backward and ignorant, and probably sub-human, and do and say stupid things.

Twenty years ago, when I was still in the "dude business," I took a middle-aged gentleman on a two-hour horseback ride. He was balding, bespectacled, perhaps a little melancholy, but a nice enough guy. In an attempt to keep things interesting, for me as well as for him, I asked what he did for a living.

"I write for television."

"No kidding!" I said.

He nodded grimly, as if it were something regrettable, and mentioned several things he had written. They ran the gamut, from sit-coms to dramas, even a couple Movies of the Week. I became immediately fired up.

"Mister," I said, "You've got a lot to answer for. I know you're not personally responsible for it, but you're as close as I'm likely to get. Explain to me why it is whenever a character on TV is supposed to be from a rural area, he's always a toothless, tobacco chewing rube."

"Because," the writer said, "the producers who run the studios honestly believe that's how it is."

"You can't be serious."

"I'm dead serious."

Starling. But, considering everything, I'm not surprised they believe it. Of course they do. It's not their fault, really. They've just bought into the same B.S. we've all been fed, year after year, decade after decade. Convenient characterizations are time-savers, because once we've got them we don't have to stop and consider actual people. And they're lots of fun, too. Aren't they! Judy Canova was hugely popular in the forties on radio, playing the goofy, gingham clad country girl with red pigtails and–as my friend John Reese once put it—an innocence so vast it was almost a form of stupidity. Simple people. Trusting people. Foolish. Think Ma and Pa Kettle. Think the Beverly Hillbillies.

On the other side of the coin, movie stars Ronald Coleman and Myrna

Loy were the constant thrust and parry of rapier wits, as were the urbane Spencer Tracy and Katherine Hepburn, and weren't they smart and wouldn't we all like to be them, so erudite and glib with such nifty wardrobes to boot? City people, smooth and classy.

Convenient characterizations. The problem is, these days the characterizations have become mean spirited. The innocent and trusting are now portrayed as idiots. The smooth and classy are depicted as arrogant and cruel. Everything has to have an edge to it. Everything has to sting.

So, we don't have television anymore. I find that this has improved my attitude and lowered my blood pressure. Because when you go out there and start walking around, there's just people. Very few Ronald Colemans, even fewer Judy Canovas. Just folks. None of them have writers feeding them dialog, witty or otherwise.

Thank goodness. I would never be able to keep up.

PIGAROO AND THE CODE OF THE WEST

BILLY WAS A horseshoer, and a big one, standing at least six foot four inches and as broad across the chest as a small storage shed, an expanse made to seem even larger by the prodigious handle-bar mustache he wore. When he waxed the points of that mustache, which he did for formal occasions like funerals and barbecues and livestock auctions, they stood nearly shoulder width. When he was working under a horse he wore a battered ball cap with sweat stains, the same as everybody else, but the rest of the time sported a black, open crown reservation-style Stetson, just a monster of a hat, which of course made him even taller. He had a loud, rolling laugh, was good with mules and knew how to throw a box-hitch and a double diamond.

Across from the saddling corrals at the Alamitos Ranch stood an L-shaped, ten-stall barn dating from back the nineteen-twenties, when the main business of the place was raising thoroughbred race horses instead of being a dude ranch. This area had been fenced off and turned into a petting zoo for the little children, and was strewn with baby goats and bunny rabbits and sheep and strange looking chickens—along with one ancient, dusty, desert tortoise. Watching over this squirming, bleating population was Myrt, the Petting Zoo Lady.

Myrt was seventy years old and called everybody "babe." When the kids came through her gate she'd say, "The ducks are over this way, babe," and, "Pet these little animals only on the body and not the head, babe," and, "Stop crying, babe, you're scaring the goats." Life and cigarettes and three failed marriages had worn her down to nothing but leather and bone and raspy voice. If she weighed a hundred pounds she was soaking wet with her pockets full of rocks, but you didn't want to cross her, no sir. She'd whip that finger up and start shaking it at you, and back you into a corner, and by the time she was done you felt like you'd taken a whipping with a belt instead of a tongue lashing.

Among Myrt's charges in this menagerie were three miniature horses. I don't know where she got them, but no doubt it was the same old story—people acquire little useless animals they think are cute and adorable, then lose interest after a while, and what better place to dispose of them than the local petting zoo? Miniature horses are, I suppose, cute enough, but there is no reason on God's green earth that we should have them. Just no reason, whatsoever. They have been bred into existence by man, the same as certain tiny breeds of dogs have been bred into existence, and whoever the people are doing such things, they need to stop it.

I don't know what I'd been up to that day, but it couldn't have been very important, otherwise I'd have been somewhere else. As it was, I looked up, and across the alley in the middle of the petting zoo was Billy, all two hundred sixty pounds of him, with a teensy horse tucked up under his arm and a pair of nippers in his hand, snipping away at the tiny hooves. It was a bizarre sight, the smallest horse imaginable getting a pedicure from the largest farrier in seven counties, like something out of a Salvador Dali painting. Dainty isn't the correct word, but God help me it was the only word that kept running through my head in spite of everything I could do to stop it.

He saw me there, staring, with my mouth open, and put the little horse down in front of him. He straightened up, stretching his back, then pointed at me with the nippers.

"Hey, cowboy," he said.

Myrt stood a few feet away, smoking one of her Virginia Slims cigarettes. She was hovering, the way she did anytime somebody else messed with one of her animals. Even when it was somebody she was paying to mess with them, like Billy, it made her nervous. She gave me a wave. "Hi, babe."

Billy said to her, "Maybe this fella right here is the answer to our problem."

"Why, sure," Myrt said. "You'd help us, wouldn't you, babe?"

I said, "Help you do what?"

Billy said, "We have a pig problem."

"Say again?"

"Pigs! You know anything about pigs?"

I looked around. There wasn't a pig anywhere near them. "I don't know," I said. "Maybe."

"It's the little pot-bellied pigs, babe," Myrt said. "They need their toes trimmed back."

I immediately took one step in the opposite direction. "We raised some pigs when I was a kid. But we never had any that you needed to trim. You mean like you do a horse?"

"Billy needs help," Myrt said, "and I'm not strong enough to hold them."

"Follow me, cowboy," Billy said, and when somebody that size tells you to do something it's just natural to go ahead and do it. Plus, I'd never in my life heard of trimming a pig, and my curiosity was raised.

I climbed over the pipe rail fence, managing not to step on the desert tortoise, and all three of us went across the miniature horse pen, through a series of short, mysterious wire gates past several ducks and one mean goose that tried to nip me, and wound up at the Dutch doors to one of the old box stalls. The top hinge of the door was loose, which meant that Myrt had to lift it up and drag it open. I moved to help her and she waved me away.

"Don't let 'em get out, babe," she said.

It was dark in there, and smelled like pigs.

Now, pigs are nasty. There's a reason all those old guys in the Bible talked about them being unclean, and that's because they are. They are vile and they stink, they have bristly little hairs and beady little pig eyes, and I believe in their hearts they mean us harm. I've never liked being around them and I've damn sure never trusted one of them, not a single one. I love to eat pork chops and bacon and spare ribs the same as everybody else, maybe even more than most, but that doesn't require me to harbor warm and fuzzy thoughts about the animal that provides them. And here, among the pine shavings on the floor of this stall were two of the little turds, grunting and snuffling in the shadows, smelling like old dirty socks that had been soaked in ammonia.

Myrt pointed. "That one is named Charles, and this one is Princess Diana."

Pot-bellied pigs. Their legs are six inches long and their round bellies drag the ground, and for a brief time in history they were all the rage and everybody wanted them as pets, because as babies they're cute—that word again—as all piglets are, but sooner or later they grow up and instead of being pot-bellied pigs they turn into pot-bellied hogs, and become pushy and nasty and not so cute, and then people don't want them anymore. Just like the mini-horses they wind up in petting zoos.

I said, "What is it you want me to do?"

"Their front toes has growed over the top of each other," Billy said. "See there?"

He nodded toward the malady. I looked. "Huh," I said. "I seen some old cows whose feet grew that way, but I never knew it could happen to pigs."

"It happens to these pigs. I need you to catch them and hold them for me."

"Do what, now?"

"Hold them while I clip them."

The nearest pig, judging by the plumbing it must have been Charles, peered up at me in the harsh sunlight coming through the doorway, blinking rapidly like a near-sighted person who had mis-placed his glasses. He'd once had a set of tusks on him, but somewhere down the line someone had clipped them off. The ragged stubs still showed.

"What am I supposed to do, leg them over and sit on their heads?" The thought of those snaggly teeth under my hindquarters was not appealing.

Myrt said, "No, babe. You get behind them and pick them up backwards. You lift their front ends off the ground."

Of course she'd know about such things. I sure didn't. Not only had I never trimmed a pig, I'd never wrestled with one, either. In fact, there were certain things a cowboy should never be seen doing, and I was pretty sure that messing with pigs in any way was up there near the top of the list. I looked at Billy.

"Don't you dare tell anybody I done this."

He laughed. "Don't worry. I won't breathe a word."

"Swear," I said.

He raised a hand. "I swear. I won't tell nobody."

Well, hell. There wasn't anything to do but dive in. If you have to wrestle a pig it's best not to spend too much time thinking about it. I don't know if that's a famous saying, but it probably should be. I decided to start with Charles since he was the biggest, and I grabbed for him, but he squirted away and all I got was one hind foot. He started dragging me around the stall, jerking his leg and screaming as if I were sticking him with a red-hot poker.

Myrt hollered, "His front legs, babe, not his back ones. Let him go, he'll settle down."

He was stronger than I expected. There was a lot of muscle in those big hams, but now that I had hold of him I wasn't about to let go, which meant he was bound to duck back between my legs and turn me inside out, and that's exactly what he did, yanking me clean off my feet, and I did a face-plant into the cedar shavings, where those two royal hogs had spent most of the morning pooping. I let go.

"He'll settle down in a minute," Myrt assured me.

Billy said, "Don't give up there, cowboy." He seemed to be enjoying himself, leaning against the wall, watching.

I got up and brushed the shavings off my jeans. Maybe it would be easier with the smaller pig, Princess Diana, though I had no practical reason to think so. I scooped up one of her hind legs, but I had pig-poop on my hands and she slithered free, and started making tight, frantic circles around the inside of the stall, like she was running laps. I paced her, fixing to make another try, when Myrt gave a squawk and hung one skinny leg over the top of the princess as she rushed by, grabbed her by both front armpits and hoisted her backwards. I don't know if the place she grabbed is actually called armpits on a pig; just under the front legs, anyhow. It was a smooth, practiced move, something a guy might even admire. If it hadn't involved a pig.

Princess Diana squealed, and squealed again, and kept squealing. She was a small, piercing siren and the noise pretty much filled up the stall.

"Like this, babe," Myrt shouted over the din. "Rock her backwards!"

I was ashamed to be shown up by a scrawny little old lady no thicker than a twig who smoked cigarettes. I had a feeling that if I was the one who needed to be wrestled down and rocked back on my haunches, Myrt wouldn't have had any trouble with me, either. I cowboyed up and took over, grabbing the hog, keeping her tipped onto her hams, and she screamed and chuffed into my ear. Billy waded in, chuckling, my wasn't this amusing, and snipped away at the overgrown hooves with his horse nippers. It took only a few seconds, and when he was done I released the little demon. The screaming stopped, like you'd thrown a switch, and she scurried over to stand and snuffle next to Charles.

"If a cowboy is good at working with pigs," Billy said, "wouldn't you call him a pigaroo?" He grinned at me.

I thought, har-dee-har-har.

Between the three of us we managed to get Prince Charles wallowed up in a corner where I could get hold of him again. Quite a dust-up ensued. By the time it was over my hat was crumpled, a good straw hat I'd paid forty bucks for less than six months ago, my shirt tail was ripped and one of my sleeves had a hole in it, I had a bruise on my calf where he'd tried to take a hunk out of me but couldn't bite through my jeans, and there were shavings plastered pretty much over all of me. I looked like I'd been rolled in bread crumbs prior to frying. But those little toes were trimmed short and neat, by golly.

As we stumbled from the stall back into daylight, Myrt said, "Thanks, babe. I owe you one."

And Billy said, "Good job, pigaroo."

I flashed him a look. He laughed, slipped his nippers into the black rubber bucket that served as his tool box, climbed into his pickup and rolled away. I proceeded to the water trough and washed up a little, then went back to whatever it was I'd been doing before.

On my way into town I stopped at the post office to buy some stamps. I think it was fifty-three minutes later, not even a whole hour. I was third or forth in line, just minding my own business waiting my turn, when Jake Copass came into the lobby and spotted me. He ambled over.

Jake was around eighty, white-haired and blue-eyed, a true son of Texas with a silver belly Resistol hat and a neatly knotted neckerchief. There was nothing he liked better than a good joke, and I thought, judging from his expression, he was about to tell me one.

Instead, he said, "Excuse me, sir, but you look kindly familiar. Aren't you the world famous. . . pigaroo?"

I said, slowly, "You got to be kidding me."

Jake cackled. "The well-known pork wrangler!"

"Where did you hear about that?"

"Oh, a little bird told me."

"A little bird. I'm thinking it was a big bird. A great big bird with a handle-bar mustache."

"All I know is they tell me you was pretty handy when it comes to pigs. I never knowed that about you."

The next morning on my way to work I stopped off at Paula's Pancake House for a cup of coffee. Paula's is a little out of the way for me, you have to turn right instead of left off the highway to get there, when you're headed to the ranch, so I only go by maybe three or four times a month. But they have great coffee, and I wanted a big Styrofoam cup to go. As I waited by the cash register one of the waitresses said, "I hear you wrestle pigs."

I had no idea this person even knew what my name was. I sure didn't know her name. I said, "What?"

"That's what I hear," she said.

"Hear from where?" I said.

"Oh, around. Just around."

The next afternoon I went by the bank to check on the dwindling balance of my account, and the teller, a woman I'd dealt with for a year and a half, in two-minute increments, and who I wouldn't expect to recognize me if we met on the street, looked at me funny as she handed me back my passbook.

"I heard the strangest thing about you," she said.

"Oh?"

"Somebody said you adopted a whole herd of hogs, and were taking care of them."

"A herd?"

"Yes, a whole herd of them. Isn't that what you call it if you have a bunch of hogs? A herd?"

"I'm not sure."

"Is that what you do, are you a pig farmer? I thought you worked with horses."

"I don't have any pigs. Not even one."

"Wow. What a strange rumor. You wonder how these things get started."

"Oh," I said, "I don't wonder at all, really."

It was all over the valley. Everywhere. In the supermarket I ran into acquaintances who found it amusing to come up and say, "pigaroo," to me. At Hamley's Corner liquor store where I stopped to buy a tin of Copenhagen, the owner, a big gray-backed Danish man with a thick mustache, who I bet hadn't uttered a dozen words to me before, said, "You mind them hogs, now," as he counted out my change. People I hadn't heard from in months called me on the phone to ask about my new and sudden interest in pork. In the parking lot of the feed store a little kid I didn't even know ran up to me and called me a "pigpoke." And once, as I knelt down to take off my spurs before coming into the house, I swear somebody behind me whispered, "*Oink-oink*!" I stood up quickly and looked around, but nobody was there.

It was late afternoon a few days later when I spotted Billy's truck parked in the shade of the big oak trees outside the Red Barn Restaurant and Lounge. I parked and went inside, blinking like an owl in the dim light. I found him at the bar with a beer in front of him and his big reservation hat pushed back off his forehead.

"Hey, cowboy," he said. "Take a seat. Buy you a *cerveza*?"

"At the very least," I said.

I took the stool next to him and he waved down the bartender. I ordered a beer and it was promptly delivered. Billy raised his bottle.

"Here's looking up your old address."

We drank. Billy dabbed at his mustache with a bar napkin.

"So," he said. "Tell me. How's it going?"

"Pretty good," I said, "considering that I seem to be entertaining the whole county these days."

He nodded. "Do tell."

"That's the thing. I didn't have to tell. It's already been told for me. Pretty much everyplace."

"Ain't it amazing, the way these stories get around."

"I could swear I remember somebody gave me his word he wouldn't breath it to a soul."

Billy took another sip of his beer, another dab with the napkin. He was smiling under his handlebars. "I seem to remember that myself, now you mention it."

We drank our beers and ate some peanuts from the green plastic bowl they had there. The TV above the bar was showing the news and we watched that for a few minutes. There was nothing in the newscast about me or the pigs, so that was something. When the bartender came back around we ordered two more beers.

I said, "So how's that work? The Code of the West and all that, a man's word being his bond?"

He looked at me. "You're kidding, right?"

"I don't think so. You know. The cowboy way."

"Didn't nobody ever tell you? All that stuff goes out the window if the story is good enough."

I considered that. "Really."

He nodded. "As a matter of fact, I think it's already written into the Code of the West. It's like an official footnote, or something."

"A footnote."

"Absolutely."

"I think you are pulling my leg awful hard," I said. "I think you are so full of it your eyes are brown."

"Put it this way. Think about this. Suppose it was me crawling around down there with those hogs. You could give your word, you could swear on a stack of Bibles, whatever you wanted, but how long could you have sat on that before you blabbed it to somebody?"

We ate some more peanuts. After a while the news was over and *Wheel of Fortune* came on. Billy said, "You want another beer, Pigaroo?"

"Let me buy this round," I said.